EUGENE O'NEILL,

one of America's greatest dramatists, was born on October 16, 1888, in a hotel room on Broadway in New York City. As a teenager, he attended boarding school and was admitted to Princeton but was dismissed for misconduct during his freshman year. O'Neill then began an itinerant existence that took him on sea voyages around the world. Intending to return to the theater in his father's theatrical company, O'Neill ended up, at twenty-five, in a tuberculosis sanitarium, his vagabond life having nearly killed him. After this enforced rest he joined a group of Greenwich Village artists who summered in Provincetown on Cape Cod, and began to write plays. Many of these were produced in theaters on and off Braodway: *The Emperor Jones* (1920), *The Hairy Ape* (1922), *All God's Chillun Got Wings* (1924), *Desire Under the Elms* (1924), *The Great God Brown* (1926), and *Strange Interlude* (1928). Four of O'Neill's plays won the Pulitzer Prize for drama, and O'Neill was awarded the Nobel Prize for literature in 1936. His other great plays include *Mourning Becomes Electra* (1931), *Ah, Wilderness!* (1933), *The Iceman Cometh* (1946), *A Moon for the Misbegotten* (1952), and *Long Day's Journey into Night*, produced posthumously in 1956. Eugene O'Neill died of bronchial pneumonia in a Boston hotel room in 1953.

Beyond the Horizon
and
The Emperor Jones

by
Eugene O'Neill

BANTAM BOOKS
NEW YORK TORONTO LONDON SYDNEY AUCKLAND

A B A N T A M C L A S S I C

BEYOND THE HORIZON & THE EMPEROR JONES
A Bantam Classic Book / June 1996
PUBLISHING HISTORY
Beyond the Horizon *and* The Emperor Jones
were first published in 1920.

Cover art: *Ploughed Field* by Peter Jakob Clodt von Jürgensburg.
Tretyakov Gallery, Moscow. Courtesy of Scala / Art Resource,
New York.

ISBN 0-553-21452-7

Published simultaneously in the United States and Canada

Bantam Books are published by Bantam Books, a division of Bantam Doubleday Dell Publishing Group, Inc. Its trademark, consist-
ing of the words "Bantam Books" and the portrayal of a rooster,
is Registered in U.S. Patent and Trademark Office and in other
countries. Marca Registrada. Bantam Books, 1540 Broadway, New
York, New York 10036.

PRINTED IN THE UNITED STATES OF AMERICA

OPM   0 9 8 7 6 5 4 3 2 1

Contents

Beyond the Horizon

Characters

JAMES MAYO, *a farmer*
KATE MAYO, *his wife*
CAPTAIN DICK SCOTT, *of the bark "Sunda," her
brother*

ANDREW MAYO } *sons of* JAMES MAYO
ROBERT MAYO

RUTH ATKINS
MRS. ATKINS, *her widowed mother*
MARY
BEN, *a farm hand*
DOCTOR FAWCETT

Scenes

Act One

Act Two

Act Three

Act One

Scene 1

A section of country highway. The road runs diago-nally from the left, forward, to the right, rear, and can be seen in the distance winding toward the horizon like a pale ribbon between the low, rolling hills with their freshly plowed fields clearly divided from each other, checkerboard fashion, by the lines of stone walls and rough snake-fences.

The forward triangle cut off by the road is a section of a field from the dark earth of which myriad bright-green blades of fall-sown rye are sprouting. A strag-gling line of piled rocks, too low to be called a wall, separates this field from the road.

To the rear of the road is a ditch with a sloping, grassy bank on the far side. From the center of this an old, gnarled apple tree, just budding into leaf, strains its twisted branches heavenwards, black against the pallor of distance. A snake-fence sidles from left to right along the top of the bank, passing beneath the apple tree.

The hushed twilight of a day in May is just begin-ning. The horizon hills are still rimmed by a faint line of flame, and the sky above them glows with the crim-son flush of the sunset. This fades gradually as the action of the scene progresses.

At the rise of the curtain, ROBERT MAYO *is discov-ered sitting on the fence. He is a tall, slender young*

5

*man of twenty-three. There is a touch of the poet
about him expressed in his high forehead and wide,
dark eyes. His features are delicate and refined, leaning
to weakness in the mouth and chin. He is dressed in
gray corduroy trousers pushed into high laced boots,
and a blue flannel shirt with a bright colored tie. He
is reading a book by the fading sunset light. He shuts
this, keeping a finger in to mark the place, and turns
his head toward the horizon, gazing out over the fields
and hills. His lips move as if he were reciting
something to himself.*

His brother ANDREW *comes along the road from the
right, returning from his work in the fields. He is
twenty-seven years old, an opposite type to* ROBERT—
*husky, sun-bronzed, handsome in a large-featured,
manly fashion—a son of the soil, intelligent in a
shrewd way, but with nothing of the intellectual about
him. He wears overalls, leather boots, a gray flannel
shirt open at the neck, and a soft, mud-stained hat
pushed back on his head. He stops to talk to* ROBERT,
leaning on the hoe he carries.

ANDREW (*seeing* ROBERT *has not noticed his pres-
    ence—in a loud shout*):   Hey there! (ROBERT *turns
    with a start. Seeing who it is, he smiles*) Gosh, you
    do take the prize for day-dreaming! And I see you've
    toted one of the old books along with you. (*He
    crosses the ditch and sits on the fence near his
    brother*) What is it this time—poetry, I'll bet. (*He
    reaches for the book*) Let me see.
ROBERT (*handing it to him rather reluctantly*):   Look
    out you don't get it full of dirt.
ANDREW (*glancing at his hands*):   That isn't dirt—it's
    good clean earth. (*He turns over the pages. His eyes
    read something and he gives an exclamation of dis-
    gust*) Hump! (*With a provoking grin at his brother
    he reads aloud in a doleful, sing-song voice*) "I have

loved wind and light and the bright sea. But Holy and most sacred night, not as I love and have loved thee." (*He hands the book back*) Here! Take it and bury it. I suppose it's that year in college gave you a liking for that kind of stuff. I'm darn glad I stopped at high school, or maybe I'd been crazy too. (*He grins and slaps* ROBERT *on the back affectionately*) Imagine me reading poetry and plowing at the same time. The team'd run away, I'll bet.

ROBERT (*laughing*): Or picture me plowing.

ANDREW: You should have gone back to college last fall, like I know you wanted to. You're fitted for that sort of thing—just as I ain't.

ROBERT: You know why I didn't go back, Andy. Pa didn't like the idea, even if he didn't say so; and I know he wanted the money to use improving the farm. And besides, I'm not keen on being a student, just because you see me reading books all the time. What I want to do now is keep on moving so that I won't take root in any one place.

ANDREW: Well, the trip you're leaving on tomorrow will keep you moving all right. (*At this mention of the trip they both fall silent. There is a pause. Finally* ANDREW *goes on, awkwardly, attempting to speak casually*) Uncle says you'll be gone three years.

ROBERT: About that, he figures.

ANDREW (*moodily*): That's a long time.

ROBERT: Not so long when you come to consider it. You know the "Sunda" sails around the Horn for Yokohama first, and that's a long voyage on a sailing ship; and if we go to any of the other places Uncle Dick mentions—India, or Australia, or South Africa, or South America—they'll be long voyages, too.

ANDREW: You can have all those foreign parts for all of me. (*After a pause*) Ma's going to miss you a lot, Rob.

ROBERT: Yes—and I'll miss her.

ANDREW: And Pa ain't feeling none too happy to have you go—though he's been trying not to show it.

ROBERT: I can see how he feels.

ANDREW: And you can bet that I'm not giving any cheers about it. (*He puts one hand on the fence near* ROBERT.)

ROBERT (*putting one hand on top of* ANDREW'S *with a gesture almost of shyness*): I know that, too, Andy.

ANDREW: I'll miss you as much as anybody, I guess. You see, you and I ain't like most brothers—always fighting and separated a lot of the time, while we've always been together—just the two of us. It's different with us. That's why it hits so hard, I guess.

ROBERT (*with feeling*): It's just as hard for me, Andy—believe that! I hate to leave you and the old folks—but—I feel I've got to. There's something calling me— (*He points to the horizon*) Oh, I can't just explain it to you, Andy.

ANDREW: No need to, Rob. (*Angry at himself*) Hell! You want to go—that's all there is to it; and I wouldn't have you miss this chance for the world.

ROBERT: It's fine of you to feel that way, Andy.

ANDREW: Huh! I'd be a nice son-of-a-gun if I didn't, wouldn't I? When I know how you need this sea trip to make a new man of you—in the body, I mean—and give you your full health back.

ROBERT (*a trifle impatiently*): All of you seem to keep harping on my health. You were so used to seeing me lying around the house in the old days that you never will get over the notion that I'm a chronic invalid. You don't realize how I've bucked up in the past few years. If I had no other excuse for going on Uncle Dick's ship but just my health, I'd stay right here and start in plowing.

ANDREW: Can't be done. Farming ain't your nature. There's all the difference shown in just the way us two feel about the farm. You—well, you like the home part of it, I expect; but as a place to work and grow things, you hate it. Ain't that right?

ROBERT: Yes, I suppose it is. For you it's different. You're a Mayo through and through. You're wedded to the soil. You're as much a product of it as an ear of corn is, or a tree. Father is the same. This farm is his life-work, and he's happy in knowing that another Mayo, inspired by the same love, will take up the work where he leaves off. I can understand your attitude, and Pa's; and I think it's wonderful and sincere. But I—well, I'm not made that way.

ANDREW: No, you ain't; but when it comes to understanding, I guess I realize that you've got your own angle of looking at things.

ROBERT (*musingly*): I wonder if you do, really.

ANDREW (*confidently*): Sure I do. You've seen a bit of the world, enough to make the farm seem small, and you've got the itch to see it all.

ROBERT: It's more than that, Andy.

ANDREW: Oh, of course. I know you're going to learn navigation, and all about a ship, so's you can be an officer. That's natural, too. There's fair pay in it, I expect, when you consider that you've always got a home and grub thrown in; and if you're set on traveling, you can go anywhere you're a mind to without paying fare.

ROBERT (*with a smile that is half sad*): It's more than that, Andy.

ANDREW: Sure it is. There's always a chance of a good thing coming your way in some of those foreign ports or other. I've heard there are great opportunities for a young fellow with his eyes open in some of those new countries that are just being

opened up. (*Jovially*) I'll bet that's what you've
been turning over in your mind under all your qui-
etness! (*He slaps his brother on the back with a
laugh*) Well, if you get to be a millionaire all of a
sudden, call 'round once in a while and I'll pass the
plate to you. We could use a lot of money right here
on the farm without hurting it any.

ROBERT (*forced to laugh*):   I've never considered that
practical side of it for a minute, Andy.

ANDREW: Well, you ought to.

ROBERT: No, I oughtn't. (*Pointing to the horizon—
dreamily*) Supposing I was to tell you that it's just
Beauty that's calling me, the beauty of the far off
and unknown, the mystery and spell of the East
which lures me in the books I've read, the need of
the freedom of great wide spaces, the joy of wandering on and on—in quest of the secret which is
hidden over there, beyond the horizon? Suppose I
told you that was the one and only reason for my
going?

ANDREW: I should say you were nutty.

ROBERT (*frowning*):   Don't, Andy. I'm serious.

ANDREW: Then you might as well stay here, because
we've got all you're looking for right on this farm.
There's wide space enough, Lord knows; and you
can have all the sea you want by walking a mile
down to the beach; and there's plenty of horizon to
look at, and beauty enough for anyone, except in
the winter. (*He grins*) As for the mystery and spell,
I haven't met 'em yet, but they're probably lying
around somewheres. I'll have you understand this is
a first class farm with all the fixings. (*He laughs.*)

ROBERT (*joining in the laughter in spite of himself*):
It's no use talking to you, you chump!

ANDREW: You'd better not say anything to Uncle
Dick about spells and things when you're on the
ship. He'll likely chuck you overboard for a Jonah.

(*He jumps down from fence*) I'd better run along.
I've got to wash up some as long as Ruth's Ma is
coming over for supper.

ROBERT (*pointedly—almost bitterly*):   And Ruth.

ANDREW (*confused—looking everywhere except at*
ROBERT—*trying to appear unconcerned*): Yes,
Ruth'll be staying too. Well, I better hustle, I guess,
and—(*He steps over the ditch to the road while he
is talking.*)

ROBERT (*who appears to be fighting some strong in-
ward emotion—impulsively*): Wait a minute,
Andy! (*He jumps down from the fence*) There is
something I want to—(*He stops abruptly, biting his
lips, his face coloring.*)

ANDREW (*facing him; half-defiantly*):   Yes?

ROBERT (*confusedly*):   No—never mind—it doesn't
matter, it was nothing.

ANDREW (*after a pause, during which he stares fixedly
at* ROBERT'S *averted face*): Maybe I can guess
what—you were going to say—but I guess you're
right not to talk about it. (*He pulls* ROBERT'S *hand
from his side and grips it tensely; the two brothers
stand looking into each other's eyes for a minute*)
We can't help those things, Rob. (*He turns away,
suddenly releasing* ROBERT'S *hand*) You'll be coming
along shortly, won't you?

ROBERT (*dully*):   Yes.

ANDREW: See you later, then. (*He walks off down
the road to the left.* ROBERT *stares after him for a
moment; then climbs to the fence rail again, and
looks out over the hills, an expression of deep grief
on his face. After a moment or so,* RUTH *enters hurriedly from the left. She is a healthy, blonde, out-
of-door girl of twenty, with a graceful, slender
figure. Her face, though inclined to roundness, is
undeniably pretty, its large eyes of a deep blue set
off strikingly by the sun-bronzed complexion. Her*

small, regular features are marked by a certain strength—an underlying, stubborn fixity of purpose hidden in the frankly appealing charm of her fresh youthfulness. She wears a simple white dress but no hat.)

RUTH (*seeing him*):   Hello, Rob!

ROBERT (*startled*):   Hello, Ruth!

RUTH (*jumps the ditch and perches on the fence beside him*):   I was looking for you.

ROBERT (*pointedly*):   Andy just left here.

RUTH: I know. I met him on the road a second ago. He told me you were here. (*Tenderly playful*) I wasn't looking for Andy, Smarty, if that's what you mean. I was looking for *you*.

ROBERT: Because I'm going away tomorrow?

RUTH: Because your mother was anxious to have you come home and asked me to look for you. I just wheeled Ma over to your house.

ROBERT (*perfunctorily*):   How is your mother?

RUTH (*a shadow coming over her face*):   She's about the same. She never seems to get any better or any worse. Oh, Rob, I do wish she'd try to make the best of things that can't be helped.

ROBERT: Has she been nagging at you again?

RUTH (*nods her head, and then breaks forth rebelliously*):   She never stops nagging. No matter what I do for her she finds fault. If only Pa was still living— (*She stops as if ashamed of her outburst*) I suppose I shouldn't complain this way. (*She sighs*) Poor Ma, Lord knows it's hard enough for her. I suppose it's natural to be cross when you're not able ever to walk a step. Oh, I'd like to be going away some place—like you!

ROBERT: It's hard to stay—and equally hard to go, sometimes.

RUTH: There! If I'm not the stupid body! I swore I

wasn't going to speak about your trip—until after you'd gone; and there I go, first thing!

ROBERT: Why didn't you want to speak of it?

RUTH: Because I didn't want to spoil this last night you're here. Oh, Rob, I'm going to—we're all going to miss you so awfully. Your mother is going around looking as if she'd burst out crying any minute. You ought to know how I feel. Andy and you and I—why it seems as if we'd always been together.

ROBERT (*with a wry attempt at a smile*):   You and Andy will still have each other. It'll be harder for me without anyone.

RUTH: But you'll have new sights and new people to take your mind off; while we'll be here with the old, familiar place to remind us every minute of the day. It's a shame you're going—just at this time, in spring, when everything is getting so nice. (*With a sigh*) I oughtn't to talk that way when I know going's the best thing for you. You're bound to find all sorts of opportunities to get on, your father says.

ROBERT (*heatedly*):   I don't give a damn about that! I wouldn't take a voyage across the road for the best opportunity in the world of the kind Pa thinks of. (*He smiles at his own irritation*) Excuse me, Ruth, for getting worked up over it; but Andy gave me an overdose of the practical considerations.

RUTH (*slowly, puzzled*):   Well, then, if it isn't— (*With sudden intensity*) Oh, Rob, why *do* you want to go?

ROBERT (*turning to her quickly, in surprise—slowly*):   Why do you ask that, Ruth?

RUTH (*dropping her eyes before his searching glance*):   Because— (*Lamely*) It seems such a shame.

ROBERT (*insistently*):   Why?

RUTH: Oh, because—everything.

ROBERT: I could hardly back out now, even if I

wanted to. And I'll be forgotten before you know it.

RUTH (*indignantly*): You won't! I'll never forget— (*She stops and turns away to hide her confusion.*)

ROBERT (*softly*): Will you promise me that?

RUTH (*evasively*): Of course. It's mean of you to think that any of us would forget so easily.

ROBERT (*disappointedly*): Oh!

RUTH (*with an attempt at lightness*): But you haven't told me your reason for leaving yet.

ROBERT (*moodily*): I doubt if you'll understand. It's difficult to explain, even to myself. Either you feel it, or you don't. I can remember being conscious of it first when I was only a kid—you haven't forgotten what a sickly specimen I was then, in those days, have you?

RUTH (*with a shudder*): Let's not think about them.

ROBERT: You'll have to, to understand. Well, in those days, when Ma was fixing meals, she used to get me out of the way by pushing my chair to the west window and telling me to look out and be quiet. That wasn't hard. I guess I was always quiet.

RUTH (*compassionately*): Yes, you always were— and you suffering so much, too!

ROBERT (*musingly*): So I used to stare out over the fields to the hills, out there— (*He points to the horizon*) and somehow after a time I'd forget any pain I was in, and start dreaming. I knew the sea was over beyond those hills—the folks had told me— and I used to wonder what the sea was like, and try to form a picture of it in my mind. (*With a smile*) There was all the mystery in the world to me then about that—far-off sea—and there still is! It called to me then just as it does now. (*After a slight pause*) And other times my eyes would follow this road, winding off into the distance, toward the hills, as if it, too, was searching for the sea. And I'd promise myself that when I grew up and was strong, I'd follow that road, and it and I would find the sea together. (*With a smile*) You see, my making this trip is only keeping that promise of long ago.

RUTH (*charmed by his low, musical voice telling the dreams of his childhood*): Yes, I see.

ROBERT: Those were the only happy moments of my life then, dreaming there at the window. I liked to be all alone—those times. I got to know all the different kinds of sunsets by heart. And all those sunsets took place over there— (*He points*) beyond the horizon. So gradually I came to believe that all the wonders of the world happened on the other side of those hills. There was the home of the good fairies who performed beautiful miracles. I believed in fairies then. (*With a smile*) Perhaps I still do believe in them. Anyway, in those days they were real enough, and sometimes I could actually hear them calling to me to come out and play with them, dance with them down the road in the dusk in a game of hide-and-seek to find out where the sun was hiding himself. They sang their little songs to me, songs that told of all the wonderful things they had in their home on the other side of the hills; and they promised to show me all of them, if I'd only come, come! But I couldn't come then, and I used to cry sometimes and Ma would think I was in pain. (*He breaks off suddenly with a laugh*) That's why I'm going now, I suppose. For I can still hear them calling. But the horizon is as far away and as luring as ever. (*He turns to her—softly*) Do you understand now, Ruth?

RUTH (*spellbound, in a whisper*): Yes.

ROBERT: You feel it then?

RUTH: Yes, yes, I do! (*Unconsciously she snuggles*

close against his side. His arm steals about her as if he were not aware of the action) Oh, Rob, how could I help feeling it? You tell things so beautifully!

ROBERT (*suddenly realizing that his arm is around her, and that her head is resting on his shoulder, gently takes his arm away.* RUTH, *brought back to herself, is overcome with confusion*): So now you know why I'm going. It's for that reason—that and one other.

RUTH: You've another? Then you must tell me that, too.

ROBERT (*looking at her searchingly. She drops her eyes before his gaze*): I wonder if I ought to! You'll promise not to be angry—whatever it is?

RUTH (*softly, her face still averted*): Yes, I promise.

ROBERT (*simply*): I love you. That's the other reason.

RUTH (*hiding her face in her hands*): Oh, Rob!

ROBERT: I wasn't going to tell you, but I feel I have to. It can't matter now that I'm going so far away, and for so long—perhaps forever. I've loved you all these years, but the realization never came 'til I agreed to go away with Uncle Dick. Then I thought of leaving you, and the pain of that thought revealed to me in a flash—that I loved you, had loved you as long as I could remember. (*He gently pulls one of* RUTH'S *hands away from her face*) You mustn't mind my telling you this, Ruth. I realize how impossible it all is—and I understand; for the revelation of my own love seemed to open my eyes to the love of others. I saw Andy's love for you—and I knew that you must love him.

RUTH (*breaking out stormily*): I don't! I don't love Andy! I don't! (ROBERT *stares at her in stupid astonishment.* RUTH *weeps hysterically*) Whatever—put such a fool notion into—into your head? (*She suddenly throws her arms about his neck and hides her head on his shoulder*) Oh, Rob! Don't go away!

Please! You mustn't, now! You can't! I won't let
you! It'd break my—my heart!

ROBERT (*the expression of stupid bewilderment giving
way to one of overwhelming joy. He presses her
close to him—slowly and tenderly*):   Do you mean
that—that you love me?

RUTH (*sobbing*):   Yes, yes—of course I do—what
d'you s'pose? (*She lifts up her head and looks into
his eyes with a tremulous smile*) You stupid thing!
(*He kisses her*) I've loved you right along.

ROBERT (*mystified*):   But you and Andy were always
together!

RUTH: Because you never seemed to want to go any
place with me. You were always reading an old
book, and not paying any attention to me. I was
too proud to let you see I cared because I thought
the year you had away to college had made you
stuck-up, and you thought yourself too educated to
waste any time on me.

ROBERT (*kissing her*):   And I was thinking— (*With a
laugh*) What fools we've both been!

RUTH (*overcome by a sudden fear*):   You won't go
away on the trip, will you, Rob? You'll tell them
you can't go on account of me, won't you? You
can't go now! You can't!

ROBERT (*bewildered*):   Perhaps—you can come too.

RUTH: Oh, Rob, don't be so foolish. You know I
can't. Who'd take care of Ma? Don't you see I
couldn't go—on her account? (*She clings to him imploringly*) Please don't go—not now. Tell them
you've decided not to. They won't mind. I know
your mother and father'll be glad. They'll all be.
They don't want you to go so far away from them.
Please, Rob! We'll be so happy here together where
it's natural and we know things. Please tell me you
won't go!

ROBERT (*face to face with a definite, final decision,*

betrays the conflict going on within him): But—
Ruth—I—Uncle Dick—

RUTH: He won't mind when he knows it's for your
happiness to stay. How could he? (*As* ROBERT *remains silent she bursts into sobs again*) Oh, Rob!
And you said—you loved me!

ROBERT (*conquered by this appeal—an irrevocable decision in his voice*): I won't go, Ruth. I promise
you. There! Don't cry! (*He presses her to him,
stroking her hair tenderly. After a pause he speaks
with happy hopefulness*) Perhaps after all Andy was
right—righter than he knew—when he said I could
find all the things I was seeking for here, at home
on the farm. I think love must have been the secret—the secret that called to me from over the
world's rim—the secret beyond every horizon; and
when I did not come, it came to me. (*He clasps
RUTH to him fiercely*) Oh, Ruth, our love is sweeter
than any distant dream! (*He kisses her passionately
and steps to the ground, lifting* RUTH *in his arms
and carrying her to the road where he puts her
down.*)

RUTH (*with a happy laugh*): My, but you're strong!

ROBERT: Come! We'll go and tell them at once.

RUTH (*dismayed*): Oh, no, don't, Rob, not 'til after
I've gone. There'd be bound to be such a scene with
them all together.

ROBERT (*kissing her—gayly*): As you like—little
Miss Common Sense!

RUTH: Let's go, then. (*She takes his hand, and they
start to go off left.* ROBERT *suddenly stops and turns
as though for a last look at the hills and the dying
sunset flush.*)

ROBERT (*looking upward and pointing*): See! The
first star. (*He bends down and kisses her tenderly*)
Our star!

RUTH (*in a soft murmur*): Yes. Our very own star.

(*They stand for a moment looking up at it, their arms around each other. Then* RUTH *takes his hand again and starts to lead him away*) Come, Rob, let's go. (*His eyes are fixed again on the horizon as he half turns to follow her.* RUTH *urges*) We'll be late for supper, Rob.

ROBERT (*shakes his head impatiently, as though he were throwing off some disturbing thought—with a laugh*):   All right. We'll run then. Come on! (*They run off laughing as the curtain falls.*)

Act One
Scene 2

The small sitting room of the Mayo farmhouse about nine o'clock same night. On the left, two windows looking out on the fields. Against the wall between the windows, an old-fashioned walnut desk. In the left corner, rear, a sideboard with a mirror. In the rear wall to the right of the sideboard, a window looking out on the road. Next to the window a door leading out into the yard. Farther right, a black horsehair sofa, and another door opening on a bedroom. In the corner, a straight-backed chair. In the right wall, near the middle, an open doorway leading to the kitchen. Farther forward a double-heater stove with coal scuttle, etc. In the center of the newly-carpeted floor, an oak dining-room table with a red cover. In the center of the table, a large oil reading lamp. Four chairs, three rockers with crocheted tidies on their backs, and one straight-backed, are placed about the table. The walls are papered a dark red with a scrolly-figured pattern.

Everything in the room is clean, well-kept, and in its exact place, yet there is no suggestion of primness about the whole. Rather the atmosphere is one of the orderly comfort of a simple, hard-earned prosperity, enjoyed and maintained by the family as a unit.

JAMES MAYO, *his wife, her brother,* CAPTAIN DICK SCOTT, *and* ANDREW *are discovered.* MAYO *is his son* ANDREW *over again in body and face—an* ANDREW

20

sixty-five years old with a short, square, white beard.
MRS. MAYO *is a slight, round-faced, rather prim-
looking woman of fifty-five who had once been a
school teacher. The labors of a farmer's wife have bent
but not broken her, and she retains a certain refine-
ment of movement and expression foreign to the*
MAYO *part of the family. Whatever of resemblance*
ROBERT *has to his parents may be traced to her. Her
brother, the* CAPTAIN, *is short and stocky, with a
weather-beaten, jovial face and a white mustache—a
typical old salt, loud of voice and given to gesture. He
is fifty-eight years old.*

JAMES MAYO *sits in front of the table. He wears
spectacles, and a farm journal which he has been reading lies in his lap. The* CAPTAIN *leans forward from a
chair in the rear, his hands on the table in front of
him.* ANDREW *is tilted back on the straight-backed
chair to the left, his chin sunk forward on his chest,
staring at the carpet, preoccupied and frowning.*

As the curtain rises the CAPTAIN *is just finishing the
relation of some sea episode. The others are pretending an interest which is belied by the absent-minded
expressions on their faces.*

THE CAPTAIN (*chuckling*):   And that mission woman,
she hails me on the dock as I was acomin' ashore,
and she says—with her silly face all screwed up serious as judgment—"Captain," she says, "would
you be so kind as to tell me where the sea-gulls
sleeps at nights?" Blow me if them warn't her exact
words! (*He slaps the table with the palms of his
hands and laughs loudly. The others force smiles*)
Ain't that just like a fool woman's question? And I
looks at her serious as I could. "Ma'm," says I, "I
couldn't rightly answer that question. I ain't never
seed a sea-gull in his bunk yet. The next time I hears
one snorin'," I says, "I'll make a note of where he's

turned in, and write you a letter 'bout it." And then she calls me a fool real spiteful and tacks away from me quick. (*He laughs again uproariously*) So I got rid of her that way. (*The others smile but immediately relapse into expressions of gloom again.*)

MRS. MAYO (*absent-mindedly—feeling that she has to say something*): But when it comes to that, where do sea-gulls sleep, Dick?

SCOTT (*slapping the table*): Ho! Ho! Listen to her, James. 'Nother one! Well, if that don't beat all hell—'scuse me for cussin', Kate.

MAYO (*with a twinkle in his eyes*): They unhitch their wings, Katey, and spreads 'em out on a wave for a bed.

SCOTT: And then they tells the fish to whistle to 'em when it's time to turn out. Ho! Ho!

MRS. MAYO (*with a forced smile*): You men folks are too smart to live, aren't you? (*She resumes her knitting.* MAYO *pretends to read his paper;* ANDREW *stares at the floor.*)

SCOTT (*looks from one to the other of them with a puzzled air. Finally he is unable to bear the thick silence a minute longer, and blurts out*): You folks look as if you was settin' up with a corpse. (*With exaggerated concern*) God A'mighty, there ain't anyone dead, be there?

MAYO (*sharply*): Don't play the dunce, Dick! You know as well as we do there ain't no great cause to be feelin' chipper.

SCOTT (*argumentatively*): And there ain't no cause to be wearin' mourning, either, I can make out.

MRS. MAYO (*indignantly*): How can you talk that way, Dick Scott, when you're taking our Robbie away from us, in the middle of the night, you might say, just to get on that old boat of yours on time! I think you might wait until morning when he's had his breakfast.

SCOTT (*appealing to the others hopelessly*):   Ain't that a woman's way o' seein' things for you? God A'mighty, Kate, I can't give orders to the tide that it's got to be high just when it suits me to have it. I ain't gettin' no fun out o' missing sleep and leavin' here at six bells myself. (*Protestingly*) And the "Sunda" ain't an old ship—leastways, not very old—and she's good's she ever was.

MRS. MAYO (*her lips trembling*):   I wish Robbie weren't going.

MAYO (*looking at her over his glasses—consolingly*): There, Katey!

MRS. MAYO (*rebelliously*):   Well, I *do* wish he wasn't!

SCOTT: You shouldn't be taking it so hard, 's far as I kin see. This vige'll make a man of him. I'll see to it he learns how to navigate, 'n' study for a mate's c'tificate right off—and it'll give him a trade for the rest of his life, if he wants to travel.

MRS. MAYO: But I don't want him to travel all his life. You've got to see he comes home when this trip is over. Then he'll be all well, and he'll want to— to marry—(ANDREW *sits forward in his chair with an abrupt movement*)—and settle down right here. (*She stares down at the knitting in her lap—after a pause*) I never realized how hard it was going to be for me to have Robbie go—or I wouldn't have considered it a minute.

SCOTT: It ain't no good goin' on that way, Kate, now it's all settled.

MRS. MAYO (*on the verge of tears*):   It's all right for *you* to talk. You've never had any children. You don't know what it means to be parted from them— and Robbie my youngest, too. (ANDREW *frowns and fidgets in his chair.*)

ANDREW (*suddenly turning to them*):   There's one thing none of you seem to take into consideration— that Rob wants to go. He's dead set on it. He's been dreaming over this trip ever since it was first talked about. It wouldn't be fair to him not to have him go. (*A sudden uneasiness seems to strike him*) At least, not if he still feels the same way about it he did when he was talking to me this evening.

MAYO (*with an air of decision*): Andy's right, Katey. That ends all argyment, you can see that. (*Looking at his big silver watch*) Wonder what's happened to Robert? He's been gone long enough to wheel the widder to home, certain. He can't be out dreamin' at the stars his last night.

MRS. MAYO (*a bit reproachfully*): Why didn't you wheel Mrs. Atkins back tonight, Andy? You usually do when she and Ruth come over.

ANDREW (*avoiding her eyes*): I thought maybe Robert wanted to tonight. He offered to go right away when they were leaving.

MRS. MAYO: He only wanted to be polite.

ANDREW (*gets to his feet*): Well, he'll be right back, I guess. (*He turns to his father*) Guess I'll go take a look at the black cow, Pa—see if she's ailing any.

MAYO: Yes—better had, son. (ANDREW *goes into the kitchen on the right.*)

SCOTT (*as he goes out—in a low tone*): There's the boy that would make a good, strong sea-farin' man—if he'd a mind to.

MAYO (*sharply*): Don't you put no such fool notions in Andy's head, Dick—or you'n' me's goin' to fall out. (*Then he smiles*) You couldn't tempt him, no ways. Andy's a Mayo bred in the bone, and he's a born farmer, and a damn good one, too. He'll live and die right here on this farm, like I expect to. (*With proud confidence*) And he'll make this one of the slickest, best-payin' farms in the state, too, afore he gits through!

SCOTT: Seems to me it's a pretty slick place right now.

MAYO (*shaking his head*): It's too small. We need more land to make it amount to much, and we ain't got the capital to buy it. (ANDREW *enters from the kitchen. His hat is on, and he carries a lighted lantern in his hand. He goes to the door in the rear leading out.*)

ANDREW (*opens the door and pauses*): Anything else you can think of to be done, Pa?

MAYO: No, nothin' I know of. (ANDREW *goes out, shutting the door.*)

MRS. MAYO (*after a pause*): What's come over Andy tonight, I wonder? He acts so strange.

MAYO: He does seem sort o' glum and out of sorts. It's 'count o' Robert leavin,' I s'pose. (*To* SCOTT) Dick, you wouldn't believe how them boys o' mine sticks together. They ain't like most brothers. They've been thick as thieves all their lives, with nary a quarrel I kin remember.

SCOTT: No need to tell me that. I can see how they take to each other.

MRS. MAYO (*pursuing her train of thought*): Did you notice, James, how queer everyone was at supper? Robert seemed stirred up about something; and Ruth was so flustered and giggly; and Andy sat there dumb, looking as if he'd lost his best friend; and all of them only nibbled at their food.

MAYO: Guess they was all thinkin' about tomorrow, same as us.

MRS. MAYO (*shaking her head*): No. I'm afraid somethin's happened—somethin' else.

MAYO: You mean—'bout Ruth?

MRS. MAYO: Yes.

MAYO (*after a pause—frowning*): I hope her and Andy ain't had a serious fallin'-out. I always sorter hoped they'd hitch up together sooner or later. What d'you say, Dick? Don't you think them two'd pair up well?

SCOTT (*nodding his head approvingly*): A sweet, wholesome couple they'd make.

MAYO: It'd be a good thing for Andy in more ways than one. I ain't what you'd call calculatin' generally, and I b'lieve in lettin' young folks run their affairs to suit themselves; but there's advantages for both o' them in this match you can't overlook in reason. The Atkins farm is right next to ourn. Jined together they'd make a jim-dandy of a place, with plenty o' room to work in. And bein' a widder with only a daughter, and laid up all the time to boot, Mrs. Atkins can't do nothin' with the place as it ought to be done. She needs a man, a first-class farmer, to take hold o' things; and Andy's just the one.

MRS. MAYO (*abruptly*): I don't think Ruth loves Andy.

MAYO: You don't? Well, maybe a woman's eyes is sharper in such things, but—they're always together. And if she don't love him now, she'll likely come around to it in time. (*As* MRS. MAYO *shakes her head*) You seem mighty fixed in your opinion, Katey. How d'you know?

MRS. MAYO: It's just—what I feel.

MAYO (*a light breaking over him*): You don't mean to say— (MRS. MAYO *nods.* MAYO *chuckles scornfully*) Shucks! I'm losin' my respect for your eyesight, Katey. Why, Robert ain't got no time for Ruth, 'cept as a friend!

MRS. MAYO (*warningly*): Sss-h-h! (*The door from the yard opens, and* ROBERT *enters. He is smiling happily, and humming a song to himself, but as he comes into the room an undercurrent of nervous uneasiness manifests itself in his bearing.*)

MAYO: So here you be at last! (ROBERT *comes forward and sits on* ANDY'S *chair.* MAYO *smiles slyly at his wife*) What have you been doin' all this time—

countin' the stars to see if they all come out right and proper?

ROBERT: There's only one I'll ever look for any more, Pa.

MAYO (*reproachfully*): You might've even not wasted time lookin' for that one—your last night.

MRS. MAYO (*as if she were speaking to a child*): You ought to have worn your coat a sharp night like this, Robbie.

SCOTT (*disgustedly*): God A'mighty, Kate, you treat Robert as if he was one year old!

MRS. MAYO (*notices* ROBERT'S *nervous uneasiness*): You look all worked up over something, Robbie. What is it?

ROBERT (*swallowing hard, looks quickly from one to the other of them—then begins determinedly*): Yes, there *is* something—something I must tell you—all of you. (*As he begins to talk* ANDREW *enters quietly from the rear, closing the door behind him, and setting the lighted lantern on the floor. He remains standing by the door, his arms folded, listening to* ROBERT *with a repressed expression of pain on his face.* ROBERT *is so much taken up with what he is going to say that he does not notice* AN-DREW'S *presence*) Something I discovered only this evening—very beautiful and wonderful—something I did not take into consideration previously because I hadn't dared to hope that such happiness could ever come to me. (*Appealingly*) You must all remember that fact, won't you?

MAYO (*frowning*): Let's get to the point, son.

ROBERT (*with a trace of defiance*): Well, the point is this, Pa: I'm not going—I mean—I can't go tomorrow with Uncle Dick—or at any future time, either.

MRS. MAYO (*with a sharp sigh of joyful relief*): Oh, Robbie, I'm so glad!

MAYO (*astounded*):   You ain't serious, be you, Robert? (*Severely*) Seems to me it's a pretty late hour in the day for you to be upsettin' all your plans so sudden!

ROBERT: I asked you to remember that until this evening I didn't know myself. I had never dared to dream—

MAYO (*irritably*):   What is this foolishness you're talkin' of?

ROBERT (*flushing*):   Ruth told me this evening that—she loved me. It was after I'd confessed I loved her. I told her I hadn't been conscious of my love until after the trip had been arranged, and I realized it would mean—leaving her. That was the truth. I *didn't* know until then. (*As if justifying himself to the others*) I hadn't intended telling her anything but—suddenly—I felt I must. I didn't think it would matter, because I was going away. And I thought she loved—someone else. (*Slowly—his eyes shining*) And then she cried and said it was I she'd loved all the time, but I hadn't seen it.

MRS. MAYO (*rushes over and throws her arms about him*):   I knew it! I was just telling your father when you came in—and, oh, Robbie, I'm so happy you're not going!

ROBERT (*kissing her*):   I knew you'd be glad, Ma.

MAYO (*bewilderedly*):   Well, I'll be damned! You do beat all for gettin' folks' minds all tangled up, Robert. And Ruth too! Whatever got into her of a sudden? Why, I was thinkin'—

MRS. MAYO (*hurriedly—in a tone of warning*):   Never mind what you were thinking, James. It wouldn't be any use telling us that now. (*Meaningly*) And what you were hoping for turns out just the same almost, doesn't it?

MAYO (*thoughtfully—beginning to see this side of the*

argument): Yes; I suppose you're right, Katey. (*Scratching his head in puzzlement*) But how it ever come about! It do beat anything ever I heard. (*Finally he gets up with a sheepish grin and walks over to* ROBERT) We're glad you ain't goin', your Ma and I, for we'd have missed you terrible, that's certain and sure; and we're glad you've found happiness. Ruth's a fine girl and'll make a good wife to you.

ROBERT (*much moved*): Thank you, Pa. (*He grips his father's hand in his.*)

ANDREW (*his face tense and drawn comes forward and holds out his hand, forcing a smile*): I guess it's my turn to offer congratulations, isn't it?

ROBERT (*with a startled cry when his brother appears before him so suddenly*): Andy! (*Confused*) Why—I—I didn't see you. Were you here when—

ANDREW: I heard everything you said; and here's wishing you every happiness, you and Ruth. You both deserve the best there is.

ROBERT (*taking his hand*): Thanks, Andy, it's fine of you to— (*His voice dies away as he sees the pain in* ANDREW'S *eyes.*)

ANDREW (*giving his brother's hand a final grip*): Good luck to you both! (*He turns away and goes back to the rear where he bends over the lantern, fumbling with it to hide his emotion from the others.*)

MRS. MAYO (*to the* CAPTAIN, *who has been too flabbergasted by* ROBERT'S *decision to say a word*): What's the matter, Dick? Aren't you going to congratulate Robbie?

SCOTT (*embarrassed*): Of course I be! (*He gets to his feet and shakes* ROBERT'S *hand, muttering a vague*) Luck to you, boy. (*He stands beside* ROBERT *as if he wanted to say something more but doesn't know how to go about it.*)

ROBERT: Thanks, Uncle Dick.

SCOTT: So you're not acomin' on the "Sunda" with me? (*His voice indicates disbelief.*)

ROBERT: I can't, Uncle—not now. I wouldn't miss it for anything in the world under any other circumstances. (*He sighs unconsciously*) But you see I've found—a bigger dream. (*Then with joyous high spirits*) I want you all to understand one thing—I'm not going to be a loafer on your hands any longer. This means the beginning of a new life for me in every way. I'm going to settle right down and take a real interest in the farm, and do my share. I'll prove to you, Pa, that I'm as good a Mayo as you are—or Andy, when I want to be.

MAYO (*kindly but skeptically*):   That's the right spirit, Robert. Ain't none of us doubts your willin'ness, but you ain't never learned—

ROBERT: Then I'm going to start learning right away, and you'll teach me, won't you?

MAYO (*mollifyingly*):   Of course I will, boy, and be glad to, only you'd best go easy at first.

SCOTT (*who has listened to this conversation in mingled consternation and amazement*):   You don't mean to tell me you're going to let him stay, do you, James?

MAYO: Why, things bein' as they be, Robert's free to do as he's a mind to.

MRS. MAYO: *Let him!* The very idea!

SCOTT (*more and more ruffled*):   Then all I got to say is, you're a soft, weak-willed critter to be permittin' a boy—and women, too—to be layin' your course for you wherever they damn pleases.

MAYO (*slyly amused*):   It's just the same with me as 'twas with you, Dick. You can't order the tides on the seas to suit you, and I ain't pretendin' I can reg'late love for young folks.

SCOTT (*scornfully*):   Love! They ain't old enough to

know love when they sight it! Love! I'm ashamed of you, Robert, to go lettin' a little huggin' and kissin' in the dark spile your chances to make a man out o' yourself. It ain't common sense—no siree, it ain't—not by a hell of a sight! (*He pounds the table with his fists in exasperation.*)

MRS. MAYO (*laughing provokingly at her brother*): A fine one you are to be talking about love, Dick—an old cranky bachelor like you. Goodness sakes!

SCOTT (*exasperated by their joking*): I've never been a damn fool like most, if that's what you're steerin' at.

MRS. MAYO (*tauntingly*): Sour grapes, aren't they, Dick? (*She laughs.* ROBERT *and his father chuckle.* SCOTT *sputters with annoyance*) Good gracious, Dick, you do act silly, flying into a temper over nothing.

SCOTT (*indignantly*): Nothin'! You talk as if I wasn't concerned nohow in this here business. Seems to me I've got a right to have my say. Ain't I made all arrangements with the owners and stocked up with some special grub all on Robert's account?

ROBERT: You've been fine, Uncle Dick; and I appreciate it. Truly.

MAYO: 'Course; we all does, Dick.

SCOTT (*unplacated*): I've been countin' sure on havin' Robert for company on this vige—to sorta talk to and show things to, and teach, kinda, and I got my mind so set on havin' him I'm goin' to be double lonesome this vige. (*He pounds on the table, attempting to cover up this confession of weakness*) Darn all this silly lovin' business, anyway. (*Irritably*) But all this talk ain't tellin' me what I'm to do with that sta'b'd cabin I fixed up. It's all painted white, an' a bran new mattress on the bunk, 'n' new sheets 'n' blankets 'n' things. And Chips built in a bookcase so's Robert could take his books along—with a slidin' bar fixed across't it, mind, so's they couldn't fall out no matter how she rolled. (*With excited consternation*) What d'you suppose my officers is goin' to think when there's no one comes aboard to occupy that sta'b'd cabin? And the men what did the work on it—what'll *they* think? (*He shakes his finger indignantly*) They're liable as not to suspicion it was a *woman* I'd planned to ship along, and that she gave me the go-by at the last moment! (*He wipes his perspiring brow in anguish at this thought*) Gawd A'mighty! They're only lookin' to have the laugh on me for something like that. They're liable to b'lieve anything, those fellers is!

MAYO (*with a wink*):   Then there's nothing to it but for you to get right out and hunt up a wife somewheres for that spick 'n' span cabin. She'll have to be a pretty one, too, to match it. (*He looks at his watch with exaggerated concern*) You ain't got much time to find her, Dick.

SCOTT (*as the others smile—sulkily*):   You kin go to thunder, Jim Mayo!

ANDREW (*comes forward from where he has been standing by the door, rear, brooding. His face is set in a look of grim determination*):   You needn't worry about that spare cabin, Uncle Dick, if you've a mind to take me in Robert's place.

ROBERT (*turning to him quickly*):   Andy! (*He sees at once the fixed resolve in his brother's eyes, and realizes immediately the reason for it—in consternation*) Andy, you mustn't!

ANDREW: You've made your decision, Rob, and now I've made mine. You're out of this, remember.

ROBERT (*hurt by his brother's tone*):   But Andy—

ANDREW: Don't interfere, Rob—that's all I ask. (*Turning to his uncle*) You haven't answered my question, Uncle Dick.

SCOTT (*clearing his throat, with an uneasy side glance at* JAMES MAYO *who is staring at his elder son as if he thought he had suddenly gone mad*): O' course, I'd be glad to have you, Andy.

ANDREW: It's settled then. I can pack the little I want to take in a few minutes.

MRS. MAYO: Don't be a fool, Dick. Andy's only joking you.

SCOTT (*disgruntedly*): It's hard to tell who's jokin' and who's not in this house.

ANDREW (*firmly*): I'm not joking, Uncle Dick. (*As* SCOTT *looks at him uncertainly*) You needn't be afraid I'll go back on my word.

ROBERT (*hurt by the insinuation he feels in* ANDREW'S *tone*): Andy! That isn't fair!

MAYO (*frowning*): Seems to me this ain't no subject to joke over—not for Andy.

ANDREW (*facing his father*): I agree with you, Pa, and I tell you again, once and for all, that I've made up my mind to go.

MAYO (*dumbfounded—unable to doubt the determination in* ANDREW'S *voice—helplessly*): But why, son? Why?

ANDREW (*evasively*): I've always wanted to go.

ROBERT: Andy!

ANDREW (*half angrily*): You shut up, Rob! (*Turning to his father again*) I didn't ever mention it because as long as Rob was going I knew it was no use; but now Rob's staying on here, there isn't any reason for me not to go.

MAYO (*breathing hard*): No reason? Can you stand there and say that to me, Andrew?

MRS. MAYO (*hastily—seeing the gathering storm*): He doesn't mean a word of it, James.

MAYO (*making a gesture to her to keep silence*): Let me talk, Katey. (*In a more kindly tone*) What's come over you so sudden, Andy? You know's well as I do that it wouldn't be fair o' you to run off at a moment's notice right now when we're up to our necks in hard work.

ANDREW (*avoiding his eyes*):   Rob'll hold his end up as soon as he learns.

MAYO: Robert was never cut out for a farmer, and you was.

ANDREW: You can easily get a man to do my work.

MAYO (*restraining his anger with an effort*):   It sounds strange to hear you, Andy, that I always thought had good sense, talkin' crazy like that. (*Scornfully*) Get a man to take your place! You ain't been workin' here for no hire, Andy, that you kin give me your notice to quit like you've done. The farm is your'n as well as mine. You've always worked on it with that understanding; and what you're sayin' you intend doin' is just skulkin' out o' your rightful responsibility.

ANDREW (*looking at the floor—simply*):   I'm sorry, Pa. (*After a slight pause*) It's no use talking any more about it.

MRS. MAYO (*in relief*):   There! I knew Andy'd come to his senses!

ANDREW: Don't get the wrong idea, Ma. I'm not backing out.

MAYO: You mean you're goin' in spite of—everythin'?

ANDREW: Yes. I'm going. I've got to. (*He looks at his father defiantly*) I feel I oughtn't to miss this chance to go out into the world and see things, and—I want to go.

MAYO (*with bitter scorn*):   So—you want to go out into the world and see thin's? (*His voice raised and quivering with anger*) I never thought I'd live to see the day when a son o' mine'd look me in the face and tell a bare-faced lie! (*Bursting out*) You're a liar, Andy Mayo, and a mean one to boot!

MRS. MAYO: James!

ROBERT: Pa!

SCOTT: Steady there, Jim!

MAYO (*waving their protests aside*): He is and he knows it.

ANDREW (*his face flushed*): I won't argue with you, Pa. You can think as badly of me as you like.

MAYO (*shaking his finger at* ANDY, *in a cold rage*): You know I'm speakin' truth—that's why you're afraid to argy! You lie when you say you want to go 'way—and see thin's! You ain't got no likin' in the world to go. I've watched you grow up, and I know your ways, and they're my ways. You're runnin' against your own nature, and you're goin' to be a'mighty sorry for it if you do. 'S if I didn't know your real reason for runnin' away! And runnin' away's the only words to fit it. You're runnin' away 'cause you're put out and riled 'cause your own brother's got Ruth 'stead o' you, and—

ANDREW (*his face crimson—tensely*): Stop, Pa! I won't stand hearing that—not even from you!

MRS. MAYO (*rushing to* ANDY *and putting her arms about him protectingly*): Don't mind him, Andy dear. He don't mean a word he's saying! (ROBERT *stands rigidly, his hands clenched, his face contracted by pain.* SCOTT *sits dumbfounded and openmouthed.* ANDREW *soothes his mother who is on the verge of tears.*)

MAYO (*in angry triumph*): It's the truth, Andy Mayo! And you ought to be bowed in shame to think of it!

ROBERT (*protestingly*): Pa!

MRS. MAYO (*coming from* ANDREW *to his father; puts her hands on his shoulders as though to try to push him back in the chair from which he has risen*): Won't you be still, James? Please won't you?

MAYO (*looking at* ANDREW *over his wife's shoulder—stubbornly*): The truth—God's truth!

MRS. MAYO: Sh-h-h! (*She tries to put a finger across his lips, but he twists his head away.*)

ANDREW (*who has regained control over himself*): You're wrong, Pa, it isn't truth. (*With defiant assertiveness*) I don't love Ruth. I never loved her, and the thought of such a thing never entered my head.

MAYO (*with an angry snort of disbelief*): Hump! You're pilin' lie on lie.

ANDREW (*losing his temper—bitterly*): I suppose it'd be hard for you to explain anyone's wanting to leave this blessed farm except for some outside reason like that. But I'm sick and tired of it—whether you want to believe me or not—and that's why I'm glad to get a chance to move on.

ROBERT: Andy! Don't! You're only making it worse.

ANDREW (*sulkily*): I don't care. I've done my share of work here. I've earned my right to quit when I want to. (*Suddenly overcome with anger and grief; with rising intensity*) I'm sick and tired of the whole damn business. I hate the farm and every inch of ground in it. I'm sick of digging in the dirt and sweating in the sun like a slave without getting a word of thanks for it. (*Tears of rage starting to his eyes—hoarsely*) I'm through, through for good and all; and if Uncle Dick won't take me on his ship, I'll find another. I'll get away somewhere, somehow.

MRS. MAYO (*in a frightened voice*): Don't you answer him, James. He doesn't know what he's saying. Don't say a word to him 'til he's in his right senses again. Please James, don't—

MAYO (*pushes her away from him; his face is drawn and pale with the violence of his passion. He glares at* ANDREW *as if he hated him*): You dare to—you dare to speak like that to me? You talk like that 'bout this farm—the Mayo farm—where you was born—you—you— (*He clenches his fist above his head and advances threateningly on* ANDREW) You damned whelp!

MRS. MAYO (*with a shriek*): James! (*She covers her face with her hands and sinks weakly into* MAYO'S *chair.* ANDREW *remains standing motionless, his face pale and set.*)

SCOTT (*starting to his feet and stretching his arms across the table toward* MAYO): Easy there, Jim!

ROBERT (*throwing himself between father and brother*): Stop! Are you mad?

MAYO (*grabs* ROBERT'S *arm and pushes him aside— then stands for a moment gasping for breath before* ANDREW. *He points to the door with a shaking finger*): Yes—go—go!— You're no son o' mine—no son o' mine! You can go to hell if you want to! Don't let me find you here—in the mornin'—or— or—I'll *throw* you out!

ROBERT: Pa! For God's sake! (MRS. MAYO *bursts into noisy sobbing.*)

MAYO (*he gulps convulsively and glares at* ANDREW): You go—tomorrow mornin'—and by God—don't come back—don't dare come back—by God, not while I'm livin'—or I'll—I'll (*He shakes over his muttered threat and strides toward the door rear, right.*)

MRS. MAYO (*rising and throwing her arms around him—hysterically*): James! James! Where are you going?

MAYO (*incoherently*): I'm goin'—to bed, Katey. It's late, Katey—it's late. (*He goes out.*)

MRS. MAYO (*following him, pleading hysterically*): James! Take back what you've said to Andy. James! (*She follows him out.* ROBERT *and the* CAPTAIN *stare after them with horrified eyes.* ANDREW *stands rigidly looking straight in front of him, his fists clenched at his sides.*)

SCOTT (*the first to find his voice—with an explosive sigh*):   Well, if he ain't the devil himself when he's roused! You oughtn't to have talked to him that way, Andy, 'bout the damn farm, knowin' how touchy he is about it. (*With another sigh*) Well, you won't mind what he's said in anger. He'll be sorry for it when he's calmed down a bit.

ANDREW (*in a dead voice*):   You don't know him. (*Defiantly*) What's said is said and can't be unsaid; and I've chosen.

ROBERT (*with violent protest*):   Andy! You can't go! This is all so stupid—and terrible!

ANDREW (*coldly*):   I'll talk to you in a minute, Rob. (*Crushed by his brother's attitude* ROBERT *sinks down into a chair, holding his head in his hands.*)

SCOTT (*comes and slaps* ANDREW *on the back*):   I'm damned glad you're shippin' on, Andy. I like your spirit, and the way you spoke up to him. (*Lowering his voice to a cautious whisper*) The sea's the place for a young feller like you that isn't half dead 'n' alive. (*He gives* ANDY *a final approving slap*) You 'n' me'll get along like twins, see if we don't. I'm goin' aloft to turn in. Don't forget to pack your dunnage. And git some sleep, if you kin. We'll want to sneak out extra early b'fore they're up. It'll do away with more argyments. Robert can drive us down to the town, and bring back the team. (*He goes to the door in the rear, left*) Well, good night.

ANDREW: Good night. (SCOTT *goes out. The two brothers remain silent for a moment. Then* ANDREW *comes over to his brother and puts a hand on his back. He speaks in a low voice, full of feeling*) Buck up, Rob. It ain't any use crying over spilt milk; and it'll all turn out for the best—let's hope. It couldn't be helped—what's happened.

ROBERT (*wildly*):   But it's a lie, Andy, a lie!

ANDREW: Of course it's a lie. You know it and I know it, —but that's all ought to know it.

ROBERT: Pa'll never forgive you. Oh, the whole affair is so senseless—and tragic. Why did you think you must go away?

ANDREW: You know better than to ask that. You know why. (*Fiercely*) I can wish you and Ruth all the good luck in the world, and I do, and I mean it; but you can't expect me to stay around here and watch you two together, day after day—and me alone. I couldn't stand it—not after all the plans I'd made to happen on this place thinking— (*His voice breaks*) thinking she cared for me.

ROBERT (*putting a hand on his brother's arm*): God! It's horrible! I feel so guilty—to think that I should be the cause of your suffering, after we've been such pals all our lives. If I could have foreseen what'd happen, I swear to you I'd have never said a word to Ruth. I swear I wouldn't have, Andy!

ANDREW: I know you wouldn't; and that would've been worse, for Ruth would've suffered then. (*He pats his brother's shoulder*) It's best as it is. It had to be, and I've got to stand the gaff, that's all. Pa'll see how I felt—after a time. (*As* ROBERT *shakes his head*)—and if he don't—well, it can't be helped.

ROBERT: But think of Ma! God, Andy, you can't go! You can't!

ANDREW (*fiercely*): I've got to go—to get away! I've got to, I tell you. I'd go crazy here, bein' reminded every second of the day what a fool I'd made of myself. I've got to get away and try and forget, if I can. And I'd hate the farm if I stayed, hate it for bringin' things back. I couldn't take interest in the work any more, work with no purpose in sight. Can't you see what a hell it'd be? You love her too, Rob. Put yourself in my place, and remember I haven't stopped loving her, and couldn't if I was to stay. Would that be fair to you or to her? Put yourself in my place. (*He shakes his brother fiercely by the shoulder*) What'd you do then? Tell me the truth! You love her. What'd you do?

ROBERT (*chokingly*): I'd—I'd go, Andy! (*He buries his face in his hands with a shuddering sob*) God!

ANDREW (*seeming to relax suddenly all over his body—in a low, steady voice*): Then you know why I got to go; and there's nothing more to be said.

ROBERT (*in a frenzy of rebellion*): Why did this have to happen to us? It's damnable! (*He looks about him wildly, as if his vengeance were seeking the responsible fate.*)

ANDREW (*soothingly—again putting his hands on his brother's shoulder*): It's no use fussing any more, Rob. It's done. (*Forcing a smile*) I guess Ruth's got a right to have who she likes. She made a good choice—and God bless her for it!

ROBERT: Andy! Oh, I wish I could tell you half I feel of how fine you are!

ANDREW (*interrupting him quickly*): Shut up! Let's go to bed. I've got to be up long before sun-up. You, too, if you're going to drive us down.

ROBERT: Yes. Yes.

ANDREW (*turning down the lamp*): And I've got to pack yet. (*He yawns with utter weariness*) I'm as tired as if I'd been plowing twenty-four hours at a stretch. (*Dully*) I feel—dead. (ROBERT *covers his face again with his hands.* ANDREW *shakes his head as if to get rid of his thoughts, and continues with a poor attempt at cheery briskness*) I'm going to douse the light. Come on. (*He slaps his brother on the back.* ROBERT *does not move.* ANDREW *bends over and blows out the lamp. His voice comes from the darkness*) Don't sit there mourning, Rob. It'll all come out in the wash. Come and get some sleep.

Everything'll turn out all right in the end. (ROBERT *can be heard stumbling to his feet, and the dark figures of the two brothers can be seen groping their way toward the doorway in the rear as the curtain falls.*)

Act Two

Scene 1

Same as Act One, Scene 2. Sitting room of the farm-house about half past twelve in the afternoon of a hot, sun-baked day in mid-summer, three years later. All the windows are open, but no breeze stirs the soiled white curtains. A patched screen door is in the rear. Through it the yard can be seen, its small stretch of lawn divided by the dirt path leading to the door from the gate in the white picket fence which borders the road.

The room has changed, not so much in its outward appearance as in its general atmosphere. Little significant details give evidence of carelessness, of inefficiency, of an industry gone to seed. The chairs appear shabby from lack of paint; the table cover is spotted and askew; holes show in the curtains; a child's doll, with one arm gone, lies under the table; a hoe stands in a corner; a man's coat is flung on the couch in the rear; the desk is cluttered with odds and ends; a number of books are piled carelessly on the sideboard. The noon enervation of the sultry, scorching day seems to have penetrated indoors, causing even inanimate objects to wear an aspect of despondent exhaustion.

A place is set at the end of the table, left, for someone's dinner. Through the open door to the kitchen comes the clatter of dishes being washed, in-

terrupted at intervals by a woman's irritated voice and the peevish whining of a child.

At the rise of the curtain MRS. MAYO *and* MRS. AT-KINS *are discovered sitting facing each other,* MRS. MAYO *to the rear,* MRS. ATKINS *to the right of the table.* MRS. MAYO'S *face has lost all character, disintegrated, become a weak mask wearing a helpless, doleful expression of being constantly on the verge of comfortless tears. She speaks in an uncertain voice, without assertiveness, as if all power of willing had deserted her.* MRS. ATKINS *is in her wheel chair. She is a thin, pale-faced, unintelligent-looking woman of about forty-eight, with hard, bright eyes. A victim of partial paralysis for many years, condemned to be pushed from day to day of her life in a wheel chair, she has developed the selfish, irritable nature of the chronic invalid. Both women are dressed in black.* MRS. ATKINS *knits nervously as she talks. A ball of unused yarn, with needles stuck through it, lies on the table before* MRS. MAYO.

MRS. ATKINS (*with a disapproving glance at the place set on the table*):   Robert's late for his dinner again, as usual. I don't see why Ruth puts up with it, and I've told her so. Many's the time I've said to her, "It's about time you put a stop to his nonsense. Does he suppose you're runnin' a hotel—with no one to help with things?" But she don't pay no attention. She's as bad as he is, a'most—thinks she knows better than an old, sick body like me.

MRS. MAYO (*dully*):   Robbie's always late for things. He can't help it, Sarah.

MRS. ATKINS (*with a snort*):   Can't help it! How you do go on, Kate, findin' excuses for him! Anybody can help anything they've a mind to—as long as they've got health, and ain't rendered helpless like me—(*She adds as a pious afterthought*)—through the will of God.

MRS. MAYO: Robbie can't.

MRS. ATKINS: Can't! It do make me mad, Kate Mayo, to see folks that God gave all the use of their limbs to potterin' round and wastin' time doin' everything the wrong way—and me powerless to help and at their mercy, you might say. And it ain't that I haven't pointed the right way to 'em. I've talked to Robert thousands of times and told him how things ought to be done. You know that, Kate Mayo. But d'you s'pose he takes any notice of what I say? Or Ruth, either—my own daughter? No, they think I'm a crazy, cranky old woman, half dead a'ready, and the sooner I'm in the grave and out o' their way the better it'd suit them.

MRS. MAYO: You mustn't talk that way, Sarah. They're not as wicked as that. And you've got years and years before you.

MRS. ATKINS: You're like the rest, Kate. You don't know how near the end I am. Well, at least I can go to my eternal rest with a clear conscience. I've done all a body could do to avert ruin from this house. On their heads be it!

MRS. MAYO (*with hopeless indifference*): Things might be worse. Robert never had any experience in farming. You can't expect him to learn in a day.

MRS. ATKINS (*snappily*): He's had three years to learn, and he's gettin' worse 'stead of better. Not on'y your place but mine too is driftin' to rack and ruin, and I can't do nothin' to prevent.

MRS. MAYO (*with a spark of assertiveness*): You can't say but Robbie works hard, Sarah.

MRS. ATKINS: What good's workin' hard if it don't accomplish anythin', I'd like to know?

MRS. MAYO: Robbie's had bad luck against him.

MRS. ATKINS: Say what you've a mind to, Kate, the

proof of the puddin's in the eatin'; and you can't deny that things have been goin' from bad to worse ever since your husband died two years back.

MRS. MAYO (*wiping tears from her eyes with her handkerchief*): It was God's will that he should be taken.

MRS. ATKINS (*triumphantly*): It was God's punishment on James Mayo for the blasphemin' and denyin' of God he done all his sinful life! (MRS. MAYO *begins to weep softly*) There, Kate, I shouldn't be remindin' you, I know. He's at peace, poor man, and forgiven, let's pray.

MRS. MAYO (*wiping her eyes—simply*): James was a good man.

MRS. ATKINS (*ignoring this remark*): What I was sayin' was that since Robert's been in charge things've been goin' down hill steady. You don't know *how* bad they are. Robert don't let on to you what's happenin'; and you'd never see it yourself if 'twas under your nose. But, thank the Lord, Ruth still comes to me once in a while for advice when she's worried near out of her senses by his goin's-on. Do you know what she told me last night? But I forgot, she said not to tell you—still I think you've got a right to know, and it's my duty not to let such things go on behind your back.

MRS. MAYO (*wearily*): You can tell me if you want to.

MRS. ATKINS (*bending over toward her—in a low voice*): Ruth was almost crazy about it. Robert told her he'd have to mortgage the farm—said he didn't know how he'd pull through 'til harvest without it, and he can't get money any other way. (*She straightens up—indignantly*) Now what do you think of your Robert?

MRS. MAYO (*resignedly*): If it has to be—

MRS. ATKINS: You don't mean to say you're goin' to

sign away your farm, Kate Mayo—after me warnin'
you?

MRS. MAYO: I'll do what Robbie says is needful.

MRS. ATKINS (*holding up her hands*):   Well, of all the
foolishness!—well, it's your farm, not mine, and
I've nothin' more to say.

MRS. MAYO: Maybe Robbie'll manage till Andy gets
back and sees to things. It can't be long now.

MRS. ATKINS (*with keen interest*):   Ruth says Andy
ought to turn up any day. When does Robert figger
he'll get here?

MRS. MAYO: He says he can't calculate exactly on
account o' the "Sunda" being a sail boat. Last letter
he got was from England, the day they were sailing
for home. That was over a month ago, and Robbie
thinks they're overdue now.

MRS. ATKINS: We can praise to God then that he'll
be back in the nick o' time. He ought to be tired of
travelin' and anxious to get home and settle down
to work again.

MRS. MAYO: Andy *has* been working. He's head officer on Dick's boat, he wrote Robbie. You know
that.

MRS. ATKINS: That foolin' on ships is all right for a
spell, but he must be right sick of it by this.

MRS. MAYO (*musingly*):   I wonder if he's changed
much. He used to be so fine-looking and strong.
(*With a sigh*) Three years! It seems more like three
hundred. (*Her eyes filling—piteously*) Oh, if James
could only have lived 'til he came back—and forgiven him!

MRS. ATKINS: He never would have—not James
Mayo! Didn't he keep his heart hardened against
him till the last in spite of all you and Robert did
to soften him?

MRS. MAYO (*with a feeble flash of anger*):   Don't you

dare say that! (*Brokenly*) Oh, I know deep down in
his heart he forgave Andy, though he was too stubborn ever to own up to it. It was that brought on
his death—breaking his heart just on account of his
stubborn pride. (*She wipes her eyes with her handkerchief and sobs.*)

MRS. ATKINS (*piously*): It was the will of God. (*The
whining crying of the child sounds from the kitchen.
MRS. ATKINS frowns irritably*) Drat that young one!
Seems as if she cries all the time on purpose to set
a body's nerves on edge.

MRS. MAYO (*wiping her eyes*): It's the heat upsets
her. Mary doesn't feel any too well these days, poor
little child!

MRS. ATKINS: She gets it right from her Pa—being
sickly all the time. You can't deny Robert was always ailin' as a child. (*She sighs heavily*) It was a
crazy mistake for them two to get married. I argyed
against it at the time, but Ruth was so spelled with
Robert's wild poetry notions she wouldn't listen to
sense. Andy was the one would have been the match
for her.

MRS. MAYO: I've often thought since it might have
been better the other way. But Ruth and Robbie
seem happy enough together.

MRS. ATKINS: At any rate it was God's work—and
His will be done. (*The two women sit in silence for
a moment.* RUTH *enters from the kitchen, carrying
in her arms her two-year-old daughter,* MARY, *a
pretty but sickly and anemic-looking child with a
tear-stained face.* RUTH *has aged appreciably. Her
face has lost its youth and freshness. There is a trace
in her expression of something hard and spiteful.
She sits in the rocker in front of the table and sighs
wearily. She wears a gingham dress with a soiled
apron tied around her waist.*)

RUTH: Land sakes, if this isn't a scorcher! That kitchen's like a furnace. Phew! (*She pushes the damp hair back from her forehead.*)

MRS. MAYO: Why didn't you call me to help with the dishes?

RUTH (*shortly*): No. The heat in there'd kill you.

MARY (*sees the doll under the table and struggles on her mother's lap*): Dolly, Mama! Dolly!

RUTH (*pulling her back*): It's time for your nap. You can't play with Dolly now.

MARY (*commencing to cry whiningly*): Dolly!

MRS. ATKINS (*irritably*): Can't you keep that child still? Her racket's enough to split a body's ears. Put her down and let her play with the doll if it'll quiet her.

RUTH (*lifting* MARY *to the floor*): There! I hope you'll be satisfied and keep still. (MARY *sits down on the floor before the table and plays with the doll in silence.* RUTH *glances at the place set on the table*) It's a wonder Rob wouldn't try to get to meals on time once in a while.

MRS. MAYO (*dully*): Something must have gone wrong again.

RUTH (*wearily*): I s'pose so. Something always going wrong these days, it looks like.

MRS. ATKINS (*snappily*): It wouldn't if you possessed a bit of spunk. The idea of you permittin' him to come in to meals at all hours—and you doin' the work! I never heard of such a thin'. You're too easy goin', that's the trouble.

RUTH: Do stop your nagging at me, Ma! I'm sick of hearing you. I'll do as I please about it; and thank you for not interfering. (*She wipes her moist forehead—wearily*) Phew! It's too hot to argue. Let's talk of something pleasant. (*Curiously*) Didn't I hear you speaking about Andy a while ago?

MRS. MAYO: We were wondering when he'd get home.

RUTH (*brightening*): Rob says any day now he's liable to drop in and surprise us—him and the Captain. It'll certainly look natural to see him around the farm again.

MRS. ATKINS: Let's hope the farm'll look more natural, too, when he's had a hand at it. The way thin's are now!

RUTH (*irritably*): Will you stop harping on that, Ma? We all know things aren't as they might be. What's the good of your complaining all the time?

MRS. ATKINS: There, Kate Mayo! Ain't that just what I told you? I can't say a word of advice to my own daughter even, she's that stubborn and self-willed.

RUTH (*putting her hands over her ears—in exasperation*): For goodness sakes, Ma!

MRS. MAYO (*dully*): Never mind. Andy'll fix everything when he comes.

RUTH (*hopefully*): Oh, yes, I know he will. He always did know just the right thing ought to be done. (*With weary vexation*) It's a shame for him to come home and have to start in with things in such a topsy-turvy.

MRS. MAYO: Andy'll manage.

RUTH (*sighing*): I s'pose it isn't Rob's fault things go wrong with him.

MRS. ATKINS (*scornfully*): Hump! (*She fans herself nervously*) Land o' Goshen, but it's bakin' in here! Let's go out in under the trees where there's a breath of fresh air. Come, Kate. (MRS. MAYO *gets up obediently and starts to wheel the invalid's chair toward the screen door*) You better come too, Ruth. It'll do you good. Learn him a lesson and let him get his own dinner. Don't be such a fool.

RUTH (*going and holding the screen door open for*

them—listlessly): He wouldn't mind. He doesn't eat much. But I can't go anyway. I've got to put baby to bed.

MRS. ATKINS: Let's go, Kate. I'm boilin' in here. (MRS. MAYO *wheels her out and off left.* RUTH *comes back and sits down in her chair.*)

RUTH (*mechanically*): Come and let me take off your shoes and stockings, Mary, that's a good girl. You've got to take your nap now. (*The child continues to play as if she hadn't heard, absorbed in her doll. An eager expression comes over* RUTH'S *tired face. She glances toward the door furtively— then gets up and goes to the desk. Her movements indicate a guilty fear of discovery. She takes a letter from a pigeon-hole and retreats swiftly to her chair with it. She opens the envelope and reads the letter with great interest, a flush of excitement coming to her cheeks.* ROBERT *walks up the path and opens the screen door quietly and comes into the room. He, too, has aged. His shoulders are stooped as if under too great a burden. His eyes are dull and lifeless, his face burned by the sun and unshaven for days. Streaks of sweat have smudged the layer of dust on his cheeks. His lips drawn down at the corners give him a hopeless, resigned expression. The three years have accentuated the weakness of his mouth and chin. He is dressed in overalls, laced boots, and a flannel shirt open at the neck.*)

ROBERT (*throwing his hat over on the sofa—with a great sigh of exhaustion*): Phew! The sun's hot today! (RUTH *is startled. At first she makes an instinctive motion as if to hide the letter in her bosom. She immediately thinks better of this and sits with the letter in her hands looking at him with defiant eyes. He bends down and kisses her.*)

RUTH (*feeling of her cheek—irritably*): Why don't you shave? You look awful.

ROBERT (*indifferently*): I forgot—and it's too much trouble this weather.

MARY (*throwing aside her doll, runs to him with a happy cry*): Dada! Dada!

ROBERT (*swinging her up above his head—lovingly*): And how's this little girl of mine this hot day, eh?

MARY (*screeching happily*): Dada! Dada!

RUTH (*in annoyance*): Don't do that to her! You know it's time for her nap and you'll get her all waked up; then I'll be the one that'll have to sit beside her till she falls asleep.

ROBERT (*sitting down in the chair on the left of table and cuddling* MARY *on his lap*): You needn't bother. I'll put her to bed.

RUTH (*shortly*): You've got to get back to your work, I s'pose.

ROBERT (*with a sigh*): Yes, I was forgetting. (*He glances at the open letter on* RUTH'S *lap*) Reading Andy's letter again? I should think you'd know it by heart by this time.

RUTH (*coloring as if she'd been accused of something—defiantly*): I've got a right to read it, haven't I? He says it's meant for all of us.

ROBERT (*with a trace of irritation*): Right? Don't be so silly. There's no question of right. I was only saying that you must know all that's in it after so many readings.

RUTH: Well, I don't. (*She puts the letter on the table and gets wearily to her feet*) I s'pose you'll be wanting your dinner now.

ROBERT (*listlessly*): I don't care. I'm not hungry.

RUTH: And here I been keeping it hot for you!

ROBERT (*irritably*): Oh, all right then. Bring it in and I'll try to eat.

RUTH: I've got to get her to bed first. (*She goes to lift* MARY *off his lap*) Come, dear. It's after time and you can hardly keep your eyes open now.

MARY (*crying*): No, no! (*Appealing to her father*) Dada! No!

RUTH (*accusingly to* ROBERT): There! Now see what you've done! I told you not to—

ROBERT (*shortly*): Let her alone, then. She's all right where she is. She'll fall asleep on my lap in a minute if you'll stop bothering her.

RUTH (*hotly*): She'll not do any such thing! She's got to learn to mind me! (*Shaking her finger at* MARY) You naughty child! Will you come with Mama when she tells you for your own good?

MARY (*clinging to her father*): No, Dada!

RUTH (*losing her temper*): A good spanking's what you need, my young lady—and you'll get one from me if you don't mind better, d'you hear? (MARY *starts to whimper frightenedly.*)

ROBERT (*with sudden anger*): Leave her alone! How often have I told you not to threaten her with whipping? I won't have it. (*Soothing the wailing* MARY) There! There, little girl! Baby mustn't cry. Dada won't like you if you do. Dada'll hold you and you must promise to go to sleep like a good little girl. Will you when Dada asks you?

MARY (*cuddling up to him*): Yes, Dada.

RUTH (*looking at them, her pale face set and drawn*): A fine one you are to be telling folks how to do things! (*She bites her lips. Husband and wife look into each other's eyes with something akin to hatred in their expressions; then* RUTH *turns away with a shrug of affected indifference*) All right, take care of her then, if you think it's so easy. (*She walks away into the kitchen.*)

ROBERT (*smoothing* MARY'S *hair—tenderly*): We'll show Mama you're a good little girl, won't we?

MARY (*crooning drowsily*): Dada, Dada.

ROBERT: Let's see: Does your mother take off your shoes and stockings before your nap?

MARY (*nodding with half-shut eyes*):   Yes, Dada.

ROBERT (*taking off her shoes and stockings*):   We'll show Mama we know how to do those things, won't we? There's one old shoe off—and there's the other old shoe—and here's one old stocking—and there's the other old stocking. There we are, all nice and cool and comfy. (*He bends down and kisses her*) And now will you promise to go right to sleep if Dada takes you to bed? (MARY *nods sleepily*) That's the good little girl. (*He gathers her up in his arms carefully and carries her into the bedroom. His voice can be heard faintly as he lulls the child to sleep.* RUTH *comes out of the kitchen and gets the plate from the table. She hears the voice from the room and tiptoes to the door to look in. Then she starts for the kitchen but stands for a moment thinking, a look of ill-concealed jealousy on her face. At a noise from inside she hurriedly disappears into the kitchen. A moment later* ROBERT *re-enters. He comes forward and picks up the shoes and stockings which he shoves carelessly under the table. Then, seeing no one about, he goes to the sideboard and selects a book. Coming back to his chair, he sits down and immediately becomes absorbed in reading.* RUTH *returns from the kitchen bringing his plate heaped with food, and a cup of tea. She sets those before him and sits down in her former place.* ROBERT *continues to read, oblivious to the food on the table.*)

RUTH (*after watching him irritably for a moment*): For heaven's sakes, put down that old book! Don't you see your dinner's getting cold?

ROBERT (*closing his book*):   Excuse me, Ruth. I didn't notice. (*He picks up his knife and fork and begins to eat gingerly, without appetite.*)

RUTH: I should think you might have some feeling for me, Rob, and not always be late for meals. If you think it's fun sweltering in that oven of a kitchen to keep things warm for you, you're mistaken.

ROBERT: I'm sorry, Ruth, really I am. Something crops up every day to delay me. I mean to be here on time.

RUTH (*with a sigh*): Mean-tos don't count.

ROBERT (*with a conciliating smile*): Then punish me, Ruth. Let the food get cold and don't bother about me.

RUTH: I'd have to wait just the same to wash up after you.

ROBERT: But I can wash up.

RUTH: A nice mess there'd be then!

ROBERT (*with an attempt at lightness*): The food is lucky to be able to get cold this weather. (*As* RUTH *doesn't answer or smile he opens his book and resumes his reading, forcing himself to take a mouthful of food every now and then.* RUTH *stares at him in annoyance.*)

RUTH: And besides, you've got your own work that's got to be done.

ROBERT (*absent-mindedly, without taking his eyes from the book*): Yes, of course.

RUTH (*spitefully*): Work you'll never get done by reading books all the time.

ROBERT (*shutting the book with a snap*): Why do you persist in nagging at me for getting pleasure out of reading? Is it because— (*He checks himself abruptly.*)

RUTH (*coloring*): Because I'm too stupid to understand them, I s'pose you were going to say.

ROBERT (*shame-facedly*): No—no. (*In exasperation*) Why do you goad me into saying things I don't mean? Haven't I got my share of troubles trying to work this cursed farm without your adding to them? You know how hard I've tried to keep things going in spite of bad luck—

RUTH (*scornfully*): Bad luck!

ROBERT: And my own very apparent unfitness for the job, I was going to add; but you can't deny there's been bad luck to it, too. Why don't you take things into consideration? Why can't we pull together? We used to. I know it's hard on you also. Then why can't we help each other instead of hindering?

RUTH (*sullenly*): I do the best I know how.

ROBERT (*gets up and puts his hand on her shoulder*): I know you do. But let's both of us try to do better. We can improve. Say a word of encouragement once in a while when things go wrong, even if it is my fault. You know the odds I've been up against since Pa died. I'm not a farmer. I've never claimed to be one. But there's nothing else I can do under the circumstances, and I've got to pull things through somehow. With your help, I can do it. With you against me— (*He shrugs his shoulders. There is a pause. Then he bends down and kisses her hair—with an attempt at cheerfulness*) So you promise that; and I'll promise to be here when the clock strikes—and anytime else you tell me to. Is it a bargain?

RUTH (*dully*): I s'pose so. (*They are interrupted by the sound of a loud knock at the kitchen door*) There's someone at the kitchen door. (*She hurries out. A moment later she reappears*) It's Ben.

ROBERT (*frowning*): What's the trouble now, I wonder? (*In a loud voice*) Come on in here, Ben. (BEN *slouches in from the kitchen. He is a hulking, awkward young fellow with a heavy, stupid face and shifty, cunning eyes. He is dressed in overalls, boots, etc., and wears a broad-brimmed hat of coarse straw pushed back on his head*) Well, Ben, what's the matter?

BEN (*drawlingly*): The mowin' machine's bust.

ROBERT: Why, that can't be. The man fixed it only last week.

BEN: It's bust just the same.

ROBERT: And can't you fix it?

BEN: No. Don't know what's the matter with the goll-darned thing. 'Twon't work, anyhow.

ROBERT (*getting up and going for his hat*): Wait a minute and I'll go look it over. There can't be much the matter with it.

BEN (*impudently*): Don't make no diff'rence t' me whether there be or not. I'm quittin'.

ROBERT (*anxiously*): You don't mean you're throwing up your job here?

BEN: That's what! My month's up today and I want what's owin' t' me.

ROBERT: But why are you quitting now, Ben, when you know I've so much work on hand? I'll have a hard time getting another man at such short notice.

BEN: That's for you to figger. I'm quittin'.

ROBERT: But what's your reason? You haven't any complaint to make about the way you've been treated, have you?

BEN: No. 'Tain't that. (*Shaking his finger*) Look-a-here. I'm sick o' being made fun at, that's what; an' I got a job up to Timms' place; an' I'm quittin' here.

ROBERT: Being made fun of? I don't understand you. Who's making fun of you?

BEN: They all do. When I drive down with the milk in the mornin' they all laughs and jokes at me—that boy up to Harris' and the new feller up to Slocum's, and Bill Evans down to Meade's, and all the rest on 'em.

ROBERT: That's a queer reason for leaving me flat. Won't they laugh at you just the same when you're working for Timms?

BEN: They wouldn't dare to. Timms is the best farm

hereabouts. They was laughin' at me for workin' for *you*, that's what! "How're things up to the Mayo place?" they hollers every mornin'. "What's Robert doin' now—pasturin' the cattle in the cornlot? Is he seasonin' his hay with rain this year, same as last?" they shouts. "Or is he inventin' some 'lectrical milkin' engine to fool them dry cows o' his into givin' hard cider?" (*Very much ruffled*) That's like they talks; and I ain't goin' to put up with it no longer. Everyone's always knowed me as a first-class hand hereabouts, and I ain't wantin' 'em to get no different notion. So I'm quittin' you. And I wants what's comin' to me.

ROBERT (*coldly*): Oh, if that's the case, you can go to the devil. You'll get your money tomorrow when I get back from town—not before!

BEN (*turning to doorway to kitchen*): That suits me. (*As he goes out he speaks back over his shoulder*) And see that I do get it, or there'll be trouble. (*He disappears and the slamming of the kitchen door is heard.*)

ROBERT (*as* RUTH *comes from where she has been standing by the doorway and sits down dejectedly in her old place*): The stupid damn fool! And now what about the haying? That's an example of what I'm up against. No one can say I'm responsible for that.

RUTH: He wouldn't dare act that way with anyone else! (*Spitefully, with a glance at* ANDREW'S *letter on the table*) It's lucky Andy's coming back.

ROBERT (*without resentment*): Yes, Andy'll see the right thing to do in a jiffy. (*With an affectionate smile*) I wonder if the old chump's changed much? He doesn't seem to from his letters, does he? (*Shaking his head*) But just the same I doubt if he'll want to settle down to a humdrum farm life, after all he's been through.

RUTH (*resentfully*): Andy's not like you. He likes the farm.

ROBERT (*immersed in his own thoughts—enthusiastically*): Gad, the things he's seen and experienced! Think of the places he's been! All the wonderful far places I used to dream about! God, how I envy him! What a trip! (*He springs to his feet and instinctively goes to the window and stares out at the horizon.*)

RUTH (*bitterly*): I s'pose you're sorry now you didn't go?

ROBERT (*too occupied with his own thoughts to hear her—vindictively*): Oh, those cursed hills out there that I used to think promised me so much! How I've grown to hate the sight of them! They're like the walls of a narrow prison yard shutting me in from all the freedom and wonder of life! (*He turns back to the room with a gesture of loathing*) Sometimes I think if it wasn't for you, Ruth, and— (*His voice softening*)—little Mary, I'd chuck everything up and walk down the road with just one desire in my heart—to put the whole rim of the world between me and those hills, and be able to breathe freely once more! (*He sinks down into his chair and smiles with bitter self-scorn*) There I go dreaming again—my old fool dreams.

RUTH (*in a low, repressed voice—her eyes smoldering*): You're not the only one!

ROBERT (*buried in his own thoughts—bitterly*): And Andy, who's had the chance—what has he got out of it? His letters read like the diary of a—of a farmer! "We're in Singapore now. It's a dirty hole of a place and hotter than hell. Two of the crew are down with fever and we're short-handed on the work. I'll be damn glad when we sail again, although tacking back and forth in these blistering seas is a rotten job too!" (*Scornfully*) That's about the way he summed up his impressions of the East.

RUTH (*her repressed voice trembling*): You needn't make fun of Andy.

ROBERT: When I think—but what's the use? You know I wasn't making fun of Andy personally, but his attitude toward things is—

RUTH (*her eyes flashing—bursting into uncontrollable rage*): You was too making fun of him! And I ain't going to stand for it! You ought to be ashamed of yourself! (ROBERT *stares at her in amazement. She continues furiously*) A fine one to talk about anyone else—after the way you've ruined everything with your lazy loafing!—and the stupid way you do things!

ROBERT (*angrily*): Stop that kind of talk, do you hear?

RUTH: You findin' fault—with your own brother who's ten times the man you ever was or ever will be! You're jealous, that's what! Jealous because he's made a man of himself, while you're nothing but a—but a— (*She stutters incoherently, overcome by rage.*)

ROBERT: Ruth! Ruth! You'll be sorry for talking like that.

RUTH: I won't! I won't never be sorry! I'm only saying what I've been thinking for years.

ROBERT (*aghast*): Ruth! You can't mean that!

RUTH: What do you think—living with a man like you—having to suffer all the time because you've never been man enough to work and do things like other people. But no! You never own up to that. You think you're so much better than other folks, with your college education, where you never learned a thing, and always reading your stupid books instead of working. I s'pose you think I ought to be *proud* to be your wife—a poor, ignorant thing like me! (*Fiercely*) But I'm not. I hate it! I hate the sight of you. Oh, if I'd only known! If I hadn't been such a fool to listen to your cheap, silly, poetry talk that you learned out of books! If I could have seen how you were in your true self—like you are now— I'd have killed myself before I'd have married you! I was sorry for it before we'd been together a month. I knew what you were really like—when it was too late.

ROBERT (*his voice raised loudly*): And now—I'm finding out what you're really like—what a—a creature I've been living with. (*With a harsh laugh*) God! It wasn't that I haven't guessed how mean and small you are—but I've kept on telling myself that I must be wrong—like a fool!—like a damned fool!

RUTH: You were saying you'd go out on the road if it wasn't for me. Well, you can go, and the sooner the better! I don't care! I'll be glad to get rid of you! The farm'll be better off too. There's been a curse on it ever since you took hold. So go! Go and be a tramp like you've always wanted. It's all you're good for. I can get along without you, don't you worry. (*Exulting fiercely*) Andy's coming back, don't forget that! He'll attend to things like they should be. He'll show what a man can do! I don't need you. Andy's coming!

ROBERT (*they are both standing.* ROBERT *grabs her by the shoulders and glares into her eyes*):   What do you mean? (*He shakes her violently*) What are you thinking of? What's in your evil mind, you—you— (*His voice is a harsh shout.*)

RUTH (*in a defiant scream*):   Yes, I do mean it! I'd say it if you was to kill me! I do love Andy. I do! I do! I always loved him. (*Exultantly*) And he loves me! He loves me! I know he does. He always did! And you know he did, too! So go! Go if you want to!

ROBERT (*throwing her away from him. She staggers back against the table—thickly*):   You—you slut! (*He stands glaring at her as she leans back, sup-*

porting herself by the table, gasping for breath. A loud frightened whimper sounds from the awakened child in the bedroom. It continues. The man and woman stand looking at one another in horror, the extent of their terrible quarrel suddenly brought home to them. A pause. The noise of a horse and carriage comes from the road before the house. The two, suddenly struck by the same premonition, listen to it breathlessly, as to a sound heard in a dream. It stops. They hear ANDY'S *voice from the road shouting a long hail—"Ahoy there!"*)

RUTH (*with a strangled cry of joy*): Andy! Andy! (*She rushes and grabs the knob of the screen door, about to fling it open.*)

ROBERT (*in a voice of command that forces obedience*): Stop! (*He goes to the door and gently pushes the trembling* RUTH *away from it. The child's crying rises to a louder pitch*) I'll meet Andy. You better go in to Mary, Ruth. (*She looks at him defiantly for a moment, but there is something in his eyes that makes her turn and walk slowly into the bedroom.*)

ANDY'S VOICE (*in a louder shout*): Ahoy there, Rob!

ROBERT (*in an answering shout of forced cheeriness*): Hello, Andy! (*He opens the door and walks out as the curtain falls.*)

Act Two

Scene 2

The top of a hill on the farm. It is about eleven o'clock the next morning. The day is hot and cloudless. In the distance the sea can be seen.

The top of the hill slopes downward slightly toward the left. A big boulder stands in the center toward the rear. Further right, a large oak tree. The faint trace of a path leading upward to it from the left foreground can be detected through the bleached, sun-scorched grass.

ROBERT *is discovered sitting on the boulder, his chin resting on his hands, staring out toward the horizon seaward. His face is pale and haggard, his expression one of utter despondency.* MARY *is sitting on the grass near him in the shade, playing with her doll, singing happily to herself. Presently she casts a curious glance at her father, and, propping her doll up against the tree, comes over and clambers to his side.*

MARY (*pulling at his hand—solicitously*):   Dada sick?
ROBERT (*looking at her with a forced smile*):   No, dear. Why?
MARY: Play wif Mary.
ROBERT (*gently*):   No, dear, not today. Dada doesn't feel like playing today.
MARY (*protestingly*):   Yes, Dada!

62

ROBERT: No, dear. Dada does feel sick—a little. He's got a bad headache.

MARY: Mary see. (*He bends his head. She pats his hair*) Bad head.

ROBERT (*kissing her—with a smile*):   There! It's better now, dear, thank you. (*She cuddles up close against him. There is a pause during which each of them looks out seaward. Finally* ROBERT *turns to her tenderly*) Would you like Dada to go away?—far, far away?

MARY (*tearfully*):   No! No! No, Dada, no!

ROBERT: Don't you like Uncle Andy—the man that came yesterday—not the old man with the white mustache—the other?

MARY: Mary loves Dada.

ROBERT (*with fierce determination*):   He won't go away, baby. He was only joking. He couldn't leave his little Mary. (*He presses the child in his arms.*)

MARY (*with an exclamation of pain*):   Oh! Hurt!

ROBERT: I'm sorry, little girl. (*He lifts her down to the grass*) Go play with Dolly, that's a good girl; and be careful to keep in the shade. (*She reluctantly leaves him and takes up her doll again. A moment later she points down the hill to the left.*)

MARY: Mans, Dada.

ROBERT (*looking that way*):   It's your Uncle Andy. (*A moment later* ANDREW *comes up from the left, whistling cheerfully. He has changed but little in appearance, except for the fact that his face has been deeply bronzed by his years in the tropics; but there is a decided change in his manner. The old easygoing good nature seems to have been partly lost in a breezy, business-like briskness of voice and gesture. There is an authoritative note in his speech as though he were accustomed to give orders and have them obeyed as a matter of course. He is dressed in the simple blue uniform and cap of a merchant ship's officer.*)

ANDREW: Here you are, eh?

ROBERT: Hello, Andy.

ANDREW (*going over to* MARY): And who's this young lady I find you all alone with, eh? Who's this pretty young lady? (*He tickles the laughing, squirming* MARY, *then lifts her up arm's length over his head*) Upsy—daisy! (*He sets her down on the ground again*) And there you are! (*He walks over and sits down on the boulder beside* ROBERT *who moves to one side to make room for him*) Ruth told me I'd probably find you up top-side here; but I'd have guessed it, anyway. (*He digs his brother in the ribs affectionately*) Still up to your old tricks, you old beggar! I can remember how you used to come up here to mope and dream in the old days.

ROBERT (*with a smile*): I come up here now because it's the coolest place on the farm. I've given up dreaming.

ANDREW (*grinning*): I don't believe it. You can't have changed that much. (*After a pause—with boyish enthusiasm*) Say, it sure brings back old times to be up here with you having a chin all by our lonesomes again. I feel great being back home.

ROBERT: It's great for us to have you back.

ANDREW (*after a pause—meaningly*): I've been looking over the old place with Ruth. Things don't seem to be—

ROBERT (*his face flushing—interrupts his brother shortly*): Never mind the damn farm! Let's talk about something interesting. This is the first chance I've had to have a word with you alone. Tell me about your trip.

ANDREW: Why, I thought I told you everything in my letters.

ROBERT (*smiling*):   Your letters were—sketchy, to say the least.

ANDREW: Oh, I know I'm no author. You needn't be afraid of hurting my feelings. I'd rather go through a typhoon again than write a letter.

ROBERT (*with eager interest*):   Then you were through a typhoon?

ANDREW: Yes—in the China sea. Had to run before it under bare poles for two days. I thought we were bound down for Davy Jones, sure. Never dreamed waves could get so big or the wind blow so hard. If it hadn't been for Uncle Dick being such a good skipper we'd have gone to the sharks, all of us. As it was we came out minus a main topmast and had to beat back to Hong-Kong for repairs. But I must have written you all this.

ROBERT: You never mentioned it.

ANDREW: Well, there was so much dirty work getting things ship-shape again I must have forgotten about it.

ROBERT (*looking at* ANDREW—*marveling*):   Forget a typhoon? (*With a trace of scorn*) You're a strange combination, Andy. And is what you've told me all you remember about it?

ANDREW: Oh, I could give you your bellyful of details if I wanted to turn loose on you. It was all-wool-and-a-yard-wide-Hell, I'll tell you. You ought to have been there. I remember thinking about you at the worst of it, and saying to myself: "This'd cure Rob of them ideas of his about the beautiful sea, if he could see it." And it would have too, you bet! (*He nods emphatically.*)

ROBERT (*dryly*):   The sea doesn't seem to have impressed you very favorably.

ANDREW: I should say it didn't! I'll never set foot on a ship again if I can help it—except to carry me some place I can't get to by train.

ROBERT: But you studied to become an officer!

ANDREW: Had to do something or I'd gone mad. The days were like years. (*He laughs*) And as for the East you used to rave about—well, you ought to see it, and *smell* it! One walk down one of their filthy narrow streets with the tropic sun beating on it would sicken you for life with the "wonder and mystery" you used to dream of.

ROBERT (*shrinking from his brother with a glance of aversion*):   So all you found in the East was a stench?

ANDREW: *A* stench! Ten thousand of them!

ROBERT: But you did like some of the places, judging from your letters—Sydney, Buenos Aires—

ANDREW: Yes, Sydney's a good town. (*Enthusiastically*) But Buenos Aires—there's the place for you. Argentine's a country where a fellow has a chance to make good. You're right I like it. And I'll tell you, Rob, that's right where I'm going just as soon as I've seen you folks a while and can get a ship. I can get a berth as second officer, and I'll jump the ship when I get there. I'll need every cent of the wages Uncle's paid me to get a start at something in B.A.

ROBERT (*staring at his brother—slowly*):   So you're not going to stay on the farm?

ANDREW: Why sure not! Did you think I was? There wouldn't be any sense. One of us is enough to run this little place.

ROBERT: I suppose it does seem small to you now.

ANDREW (*not noticing the sarcasm in* ROBERT'S *tone*):   You've no idea, Rob, what a splendid place Argentine is. I had a letter from a marine insurance chap that I'd made friends with in Hong-Kong to his brother, who's in the grain business in Buenos Aires. He took quite a fancy to me, and what's more important, he offered me a job if I'd come back there.

I'd have taken it on the spot, only I couldn't leave Uncle Dick in the lurch, and I'd promised you folks to come home. But I'm going back there, you bet, and then you watch me get on! (*He slaps* ROBERT *on the back*) But don't you think it's a big chance, Rob?

ROBERT: It's fine—for you, Andy.

ANDREW: We call this a farm—but you ought to hear about the farms down there—ten square miles where we've got an acre. It's a new country where big things are opening up—and I want to get in on something big before I die. I'm no fool when it comes to farming, and I know something about grain. I've been reading up a lot on it, too, lately. (*He notices* ROBERT'S *absent-minded expression and laughs*) Wake up, you old poetry bookworm, you! I know my talking about business makes you want to choke me, doesn't it?

ROBERT (*with an embarrassed smile*): No, Andy, I— I just happened to think of something else. (*Frowning*) There've been lots of times lately that I wished I had some of your faculty for business.

ANDREW (*soberly*): There's something I want to talk about, Rob—the farm. You don't mind, do you?

ROBERT: No.

ANDREW: I walked over it this morning with Ruth— and she told me about things— (*Evasively*) I could see the place had run down; but you mustn't blame yourself. When luck's against anyone—

ROBERT: Don't, Andy! It *is* my fault. You know it as well as I do. The best I've ever done was to make ends meet.

ANDREW (*after a pause*): I've got over a thousand saved, and you can have that.

ROBERT (*firmly*): No. You need that for your start in Buenos Aires.

ANDREW: I don't. I can—

ROBERT (*determinedly*):   No, Andy! Once and for all, no! I won't hear of it!

ANDREW (*protestingly*):   You obstinate old son of a gun!

ROBERT: Oh, everything'll be on a sound footing after harvest. Don't worry about it.

ANDREW (*doubtfully*):   Maybe. (*After a pause*) It's too bad Pa couldn't have lived to see things through. (*With feeling*) It cut me up a lot—hearing he was dead. He never—softened up, did he—about me, I mean?

ROBERT: He never understood, that's a kinder way of putting it. He does now.

ANDREW (*after a pause*):   You've forgotten all about what—caused me to go, haven't you, Rob? (ROBERT *nods but keeps his face averted*) I was a slushier damn fool in those days than you were. But it was an act of Providence I did go. It opened my eyes to how I'd been fooling myself. Why, I'd forgotten all about—that—before I'd been at sea six months.

ROBERT (*turns and looks into* ANDREW'S *eyes searchingly*):   You're speaking of—Ruth?

ANDREW (*confused*):   Yes. I didn't want you to get false notions in your head, or I wouldn't say anything. (*Looking* ROBERT *squarely in the eyes*) I'm telling you the truth when I say I'd forgotten long ago. It don't sound well for me, getting over things so easy, but I guess it never really amounted to more than a kid idea I was letting rule me. I'm certain now I never was in love—I was getting fun out of thinking I was—and being a hero to myself. (*He heaves a great sigh of relief*) There! Gosh, I'm glad that's off my chest. I've been feeling sort of awkward ever since I've been home, thinking of what you two might think. (*A trace of appeal in his voice*) You've got it all straight now, haven't you, Rob?

ROBERT (*in a low voice*): Yes, Andy.

ANDREW: And I'll tell Ruth, too, if I can get up the nerve. She must feel kind of funny having me round—after what used to be—and not knowing how I feel about it.

ROBERT (*slowly*): Perhaps—for her sake—you'd better not tell her.

ANDREW: For her sake? Oh, you mean she wouldn't want to be reminded of my foolishness? Still, I think it'd be worse if—

ROBERT (*breaking out—in an agonized voice*): Do as you please, Andy; but for God's sake, let's not talk about it! (*There is a pause.* ANDREW *stares at* ROBERT *in hurt stupefaction.* ROBERT *continues after a moment in a voice which he vainly attempts to keep calm*) Excuse me, Andy. This rotten headache has my nerves shot to pieces.

ANDREW (*mumbling*): It's all right, Rob—long as you're not sore at me.

ROBERT: Where did Uncle Dick disappear to this morning?

ANDREW: He went down to the port to see to things on the "Sunda." He said he didn't know exactly when he'd be back. I'll have to go down and tend to the ship when he comes. That's why I dressed up in these togs.

MARY (*pointing down to the hill to the left*): See! Mama! Mama! (*She struggles to her feet.* RUTH *appears at left. She is dressed in white, shows she has been fixing up. She looks pretty, flushed and full of life.*)

MARY (*running to her mother*): Mama!

RUTH (*kissing her*): Hello, dear! (*She walks toward the rock and addresses* ROBERT *coldly*) Jake wants to see you about something. He finished working where he was. He's waiting for you at the road.

ROBERT (*getting up—wearily*): I'll go down right

away. (*As he looks at* RUTH, *noting her changed appearance, his face darkens with pain.*)

RUTH: And take Mary with you, please. (*To* MARY) Go with Dada, that's a good girl. Grandma has your dinner 'most ready for you.

ROBERT (*shortly*): Come, Mary!

MARY (*taking his hand and dancing happily beside him*): Dada! Dada! (*They go down the hill to the left.* RUTH *looks after them for a moment, frowning—then turns to* ANDY *with a smile*) I'm going to sit down. Come on, Andy. It'll be like old times. (*She jumps lightly to the top of the rock and sits down*) It's so fine and cool up here after the house.

ANDREW (*half-sitting on the side of the boulder*): Yes. It's great.

RUTH: I've taken a holiday in honor of your arrival. (*Laughing excitedly*) I feel so free I'd like to have wings and fly over the sea. You're a man. You can't know how awful and stupid it is—cooking and washing dishes all the time.

ANDREW (*making a wry face*): I can guess.

RUTH: Besides, your mother just insisted on getting your first dinner to home, she's that happy at having you back. You'd think I was planning to poison you the flurried way she shooed me out of the kitchen.

ANDREW: That's just like Ma, bless her!

RUTH: She's missed you terrible. We all have. And you can't deny the farm has, after what I showed you and told you when we was looking over the place this morning.

ANDREW (*with a frown*): Things are run down, that's a fact! It's too darn hard on poor old Rob.

RUTH (*scornfully*): It's his own fault. He never takes any interest in things.

ANDREW (*reprovingly*): You can't blame him. He wasn't born for it; but I know he's done his best for your sake and the old folks and the little girl.

RUTH (*indifferently*): Yes, I suppose he has. (*Gaily*) But thank the Lord, all those days are over now. The "hard luck" Rob's always blaming won't last long when you take hold, Andy. All the farm's ever needed was someone with the knack of looking ahead and preparing for what's going to happen.

ANDREW: Yes, Rob hasn't got that. He's frank to own up to that himself. I'm going to try and hire a good man for him—an experienced farmer—to work the place on a salary and percentage. That'll take it off of Rob's hands, and he needn't be worrying himself to death any more. He looks all worn out, Ruth. He ought to be careful.

RUTH (*absent-mindedly*): Yes, I s'pose. (*Her mind is filled with premonitions by the first part of his statement*) Why do you want to hire a man to oversee things? Seems as if now that you're back it wouldn't be needful.

ANDREW: Oh, of course I'll attend to everything while I'm here. I mean after I'm gone.

RUTH (*as if she couldn't believe her ears*): Gone!

ANDREW: Yes. When I leave for the Argentine again.

RUTH (*aghast*): You're going away to sea!

ANDREW: Not to sea, no; I'm through with the sea for good as a job. I'm going down to Buenos Aires to get in the grain business.

RUTH: But—that's far off—isn't it?

ANDREW (*easily*): Six thousand miles more or less. It's quite a trip. (*With enthusiasm*) I've got a peach of a chance down there, Ruth. Ask Rob if I haven't. I've just been telling him all about it.

RUTH (*a flush of anger coming over her face*): And didn't he try to stop you from going?

ANDREW (*in surprise*): No, of course not. Why?

RUTH (*slowly and vindictively*): That's just like him—not to.

ANDREW (*resentfully*):   Rob's too good a chum to try
   and stop me when he knows I'm set on a thing. And
   he could see just as soon's I told him what a good
   chance it was.

RUTH (*dazedly*):   And you're bound on going?

ANDREW: Sure thing. Oh, I don't mean right off. I'll
   have to wait for a ship sailing there for quite a
   while, likely. Anyway, I want to stay to home and
   visit with you folks a spell before I go.

RUTH (*dumbly*):   I s'pose. (*With sudden anguish*) Oh,
   Andy, you can't go! You can't. Why we've all
   thought—we've all been hoping and praying you
   was coming home to stay, to settle down on the
   farm and see to things. You mustn't go! Think of
   how your Ma'll take on if you go—and how the
   farm'll be ruined if you leave it to Rob to look after.
   You can see that.

ANDREW (*frowning*):   Rob hasn't done so bad. When
   I get a man to direct things the farm'll be safe
   enough.

RUTH (*insistently*):   But your Ma—think of her.

ANDREW: She's used to me being away. She won't
   object when she knows it's best for her and all of
   us for me to go. You ask Rob. In a couple of years
   down there, I'll make my pile, see if I don't; and
   then I'll come back and settle down and turn this
   farm into the crackiest place in the whole state. In
   the meantime, I can help you both from down there.
   (*Earnestly*) I tell you, Ruth, I'm going to make good
   right from the minute I land, if working hard and a
   determination to get on can do it; and I *know* they
   can! (*Excitedly—in a rather boastful tone*) I tell
   you, I feel ripe for bigger things than settling down
   here. The trip did that for me, anyway. It showed
   me the world is a larger proposition than ever I
   thought it was in the old days. I couldn't be content
   any more stuck here like a fly in molasses. It all

seems trifling, somehow. You ought to be able to understand what I feel.

RUTH (*dully*): Yes—I s'pose I ought. (*After a pause— a sudden suspicion forming in her mind*) What did Rob tell you—about me?

ANDREW: Tell? About you? Why, nothing.

RUTH (*staring at him intensely*): Are you telling me the truth, Andy Mayo? Didn't he say—I— (*She stops confusedly.*)

ANDREW (*surprised*): No, he didn't mention you, I can remember. Why? What made you think he did?

RUTH (*wringing her hands*): Oh, I wish I could tell if you're lying or not!

ANDREW (*indignantly*): What're you talking about? I didn't used to lie to you, did I? And what in the name of God is there to lie for?

RUTH (*still unconvinced*): Are you sure—will you swear—it isn't the reason— (*She lowers her eyes and half turns away from him*) The same reason that made you go last time that's driving you away again? 'Cause if it is—I was going to say—you mustn't go—on that account. (*Her voice sinks to a tremulous, tender whisper as she finishes.*)

ANDREW (*confused—forces a laugh*): Oh, is *that* what you're driving at? Well, you needn't worry about that no more— (*Soberly*) I don't blame you, Ruth, feeling embarrassed having me round again, after the way I played the dumb fool about going away last time.

RUTH (*her hope crushed—with a gasp of pain*): Oh, Andy!

ANDREW (*misunderstanding*): I know I oughtn't to talk about such foolishness to you. Still I figure it's better to get it out of my system so's we three can be together same's years ago, and not be worried thinking one of us might have the wrong notion.

RUTH: Andy! Please! Don't!

ANDREW: Let me finish now that I've started. It'll
help clear things up. I don't want you to think once
a fool always a fool, and be upset all the time I'm
here on my fool account. I want you to believe I put
all that silly nonsense back of me a long time ago—
and now—it seems—well—as if you'd always been
my sister, that's what, Ruth.

RUTH (*at the end of her endurance—laughing hysterically*): For God's sake, Andy—won't you please
stop talking! (*She again hides her face in her hands,
her bowed shoulders trembling.*)

ANDREW (*ruefully*): Seems as if I put my foot in it
whenever I open my mouth today. Rob shut me up
with almost the same words when I tried speaking
to him about it.

RUTH (*fiercely*): You told him—what you've told
me?

ANDREW (*astounded*): Why sure! Why not?

RUTH (*shuddering*): Oh, my God!

ANDREW (*alarmed*): Why? Shouldn't I have?

RUTH (*hysterically*): Oh, I don't care what you do! I
don't care! Leave me alone! (ANDREW *gets up and
walks down the hill to the left, embarrassed, hurt,
and greatly puzzled by her behavior.*)

ANDREW (*after a pause—pointing down the hill*):
Hello! Here they come back—and the Captain's
with them. How'd he come to get back so soon, I
wonder? That means I've got to hustle down to the
port and get on board. Rob's got the baby with him.
(*He comes back to the boulder.* RUTH *keeps her face
averted from him*) Gosh, I never saw a father so tied
up in a kid as Rob is! He just watches every move
she makes. And I don't blame him. You both got a
right to feel proud of her. She's surely a little win-
ner. (*He glances at* RUTH *to see if this very obvious
attempt to get back in her good graces is having any
effect*) I can see the likeness to Rob standing out all

over her, can't you? But there's no denying she's
your young one, either. There's something about her
eyes—

RUTH (*piteously*): Oh, Andy, I've a headache! I don't
want to talk! Leave me alone, won't you please?

ANDREW (*stands staring at her for a moment—then
walks away saying in a hurt tone*): Everybody
hereabouts seems to be on edge today. I begin to
feel as if I'm not wanted around. (*He stands near
the path, left, kicking at the grass with the toe of
his shoe. A moment later* CAPTAIN DICK SCOTT *enters, followed by* ROBERT *carrying* MARY. *The* CAP-
TAIN *seems scarcely to have changed at all from the
jovial, booming person he was three years before.
He wears a uniform similar to* ANDREW'S. *He is puff-
ing and breathless from his climb and mops wildly
at his perspiring countenance.* ROBERT *casts a quick
glance at* ANDREW, *noticing the latter's discomfited
look, and then turns his eyes on* RUTH *who, at their
approach, has moved so her back is toward them,
her chin resting on her hands as she stares out seaward.*)

MARY: Mama! Mama! (ROBERT *puts her down and
she runs to her mother.* RUTH *turns and grabs her
up in her arms with a sudden fierce tenderness,
quickly turning away again from the others. During
the following scene she keeps* MARY *in her arms.*)

SCOTT (*wheezily*): Phew! I got great news for you,
Andy. Let me get my wind first. Phew! God
A'mighty, mountin' this damned hill is worser'n
goin' aloft to the skys'l yard in a blow. I got to lay
to a while. (*He sits down on the grass, mopping his
face.*)

ANDREW: I didn't look for you this soon, Uncle.

SCOTT: I didn't figger it, neither; but I run across a
bit o' news down to the Seamen's Home made me
'bout ship and set all sail back here to find you.

ANDREW (*eagerly*): What is it, Uncle?

SCOTT: Passin' by the Home I thought I'd drop in an' let 'em know I'd be lackin' a mate next trip 'count o' your leavin'. Their man in charge o' the shippin' asked after you 'special curious. "Do you think he'd consider a berth as Second on a steamer, Captain?" he asks. I was going to say no when I thinks o' you wantin' to get back down south to the Plate agen; so I asks him: "What is she and where's she bound?" "She's the 'El Paso,' a brand new tramp," he says, "and she's bound for Buenos Aires."

ANDREW (*his eyes lighting up—excitedly*): Gosh, that is luck! When does she sail?

SCOTT: Tomorrow mornin'. I didn't know if you'd want to ship away agen so quick an' I told him so. "Tell him I'll hold the berth open for him until late this afternoon," he says. So there you be, an' you can make your own choice.

ANDREW: I'd like to take it. There may not be another ship for Buenos Aires with a vacancy in months. (*His eyes roving from* ROBERT *to* RUTH *and back again—uncertainly*) Still—damn it all—tomorrow morning *is* soon. I wish she wasn't leaving for a week or so. That'd give me a chance—it seems hard to go right away again when I've just got home. And yet it's a chance in a thousand— (*Appealing to* ROBERT) What do you think, Rob? What would you do?

ROBERT (*forcing a smile*): He who hesitates, you know. (*Frowning*) It's a piece of good luck thrown in your way—and—I think you owe it to yourself to jump at it. But don't ask me to decide for you.

RUTH (*turning to look at* ANDREW—*in a tone of fierce resentment*): Yes, go, Andy! (*She turns quickly away again. There is a moment of embarrassed silence.*)

ANDREW (*thoughtfully*):   Yes, I guess I will. It'll be the best thing for all of us in the end, don't you think so, Rob? (ROBERT *nods but remains silent.*)

SCOTT (*getting to his feet*):   Then, that's settled.

ANDREW (*now that he has definitely made a decision his voice rings with hopeful strength and energy*): Yes, I'll take the berth. The sooner I go the sooner I'll be back, that's a certainty; and I won't come back with empty hands next time. You bet I won't!

SCOTT: You ain't got so much time, Andy. To make sure you'd best leave here soon's you kin. I got to get right back aboard. You'd best come with me.

ANDREW: I'll go to the house and repack my bag right away.

ROBERT (*quietly*):   You'll both be here for dinner, won't you?

ANDREW (*worriedly*):   I don't know. Will there be time? What time is it now, I wonder?

ROBERT (*reproachfully*):   Ma's been getting dinner especially for you, Andy.

ANDREW (*flushing—shamefacedly*):   Hell! And I was forgetting! Of course I'll stay for dinner if I missed every damned ship in the world. (*He turns to the* CAPTAIN—*briskly*) Come on, Uncle. Walk down with me to the house and you can tell me more about this berth on the way. I've got to pack before dinner. (*He and the* CAPTAIN *start down to the left.* ANDREW *calls back over his shoulder*) You're coming soon, aren't you, Rob?

ROBERT: Yes. I'll be right down. (ANDREW *and the* CAPTAIN *leave.* RUTH *puts* MARY *on the ground and hides her face in her hands. Her shoulders shake as if she were sobbing.* ROBERT *stares at her with a grim, somber expression.* MARY *walks backward toward* ROBERT, *her wondering eyes fixed on her mother.*)

MARY (*her voice vaguely frightened, taking her father's hand*): Dada, Mama's cryin', Dada.

ROBERT (*bending down and stroking her hair—in a voice he endeavors to keep from being harsh*): No, she isn't, little girl. The sun hurts her eyes, that's all. Aren't you beginning to feel hungry, Mary?

MARY (*decidedly*): Yes, Dada.

ROBERT (*meaningly*): It must be your dinner time now.

RUTH (*in a muffled voice*): I'm coming, Mary. (*She wipes her eyes quickly and, without looking at* ROBERT, *comes and takes* MARY'S *hand—in a dead voice*) Come on and I'll get your dinner for you. (*She walks out left, her eyes fixed on the ground, the skipping* MARY *tugging at her hand.* ROBERT *waits a moment for them to get ahead and then slowly follows as the curtain falls.*)

Act Three

Scene 1

Same as Act Two, Scene 1—The sitting room of the farmhouse about six o'clock in the morning of a day toward the end of October five years later. It is not yet dawn, but as the action progresses the darkness outside the windows gradually fades to gray.

The room, seen by the light of the shadeless oil lamp with a smoky chimney which stands on the table, presents an appearance of decay, of dissolution. The curtains at the windows are torn and dirty and one of them is missing. The closed desk is gray with accumulated dust as if it had not been used in years. Blotches of dampness disfigure the wall paper. Threadbare trails, leading to the kitchen and outer doors, show in the faded carpet. The top of the coverless table is stained with the imprints of hot dishes and spilt food. The rung of one rocker has been clumsily mended with a piece of plain board. A brown coating of rust covers the unblacked stove. A pile of wood is stacked up carelessly against the wall by the stove.

The whole atmosphere of the room, contrasted with that of former years, is one of an habitual poverty too hopelessly resigned to be any longer ashamed or even conscious of itself.

At the rise of the curtain RUTH *is discovered sitting by the stove, with hands outstretched to the warmth*

*as if the air in the room were damp and cold. A heavy
shawl is wrapped about her shoulders, half-concealing
her dress of deep mourning. She has aged horribly.
Her pale, deeply-lined face has the stony lack of expression of one to whom nothing more can ever happen, whose capacity for emotion has been exhausted.
When she speaks her voice is without timbre, low and
monotonous. The negligent disorder of her dress, the
slovenly arrangement of her hair, now streaked with
gray, her muddied shoes run down at the heel, give
full evidence of the apathy in which she lives.*

*Her mother is asleep in her wheel chair beside the
stove toward the rear, wrapped up in a blanket.*

*There is a sound from the open bedroom door in
the rear as if someone were getting out of bed.* RUTH
*turns in that direction with a look of dull annoyance.
A moment later* ROBERT *appears in the doorway, leaning weakly against it for support. His hair is long and
unkempt, his face and body emaciated. There are
bright patches of crimson over his cheek bones and his
eyes are burning with fever. He is dressed in corduroy
pants, a flannel shirt, and wears worn carpet slippers
on his bare feet.*

RUTH (*dully*):   S-s-s-h! Ma's asleep.

ROBERT (*speaking with an effort*):   I won't wake her.
  (*He walks weakly to a rocker by the side of the table
  and sinks down in it exhausted.*)

RUTH (*staring at the stove*):   You better come near the
  fire where it's warm.

ROBERT: No. I'm burning up now.

RUTH: That's the fever. You know the doctor told
  you not to get up and move round.

ROBERT (*irritably*):   That old fossil! He doesn't know
  anything. Go to bed and stay there—that's his only
  prescription.

RUTH (*indifferently*): How are you feeling now?

ROBERT (*buoyantly*): Better! Much better than I've felt in ages. Really I'm fine now—only very weak. It's the turning point, I guess. From now on I'll pick up so quick I'll surprise you—and no thanks to that old fool of a country quack, either.

RUTH: He's always tended to us.

ROBERT: Always helped us to die, you mean! He "tended" to Pa and Ma and— (*His voice breaks*) and to—Mary.

RUTH (*dully*): He did the best he knew, I s'pose. (*After a pause*) Well, Andy's bringing a specialist with him when he comes. That ought to suit you.

ROBERT (*bitterly*): Is that why you're waiting up all night?

RUTH: Yes.

ROBERT: For Andy?

RUTH (*without a trace of feeling*): Somebody had got to. It's only right for someone to meet him after he's been gone five years.

ROBERT (*with bitter mockery*): Five years! It's a long time.

RUTH: Yes.

ROBERT (*meaningly*): To *wait*!

RUTH (*indifferently*): It's past now.

ROBERT: Yes, it's past. (*After a pause*) Have you got his two telegrams with you? (RUTH *nods*) Let me see them, will you? My head was so full of fever when they came I couldn't make head or tail to them. (*Hastily*) But I'm feeling fine now. Let me read them again. (RUTH *takes them from the bosom of her dress and hands them to him.*)

RUTH: Here. The first one's on top.

ROBERT (*opening it*): New York. "Just landed from steamer. Have important business to wind up here. Will be home as soon as deal is completed." (*He*

 smiles bitterly) Business first was always Andy's
motto. (*He reads*) "Hope you are all well. Andy."
(*He repeats ironically*) "Hope you are all well!"

RUTH (*dully*): He couldn't know you'd been took
sick till I answered that and told him.

ROBERT (*contritely*): Of course he couldn't. I'm a
fool. I'm touchy about nothing lately. Just what did
you say in your reply?

RUTH (*inconsequentially*): I had to send it collect.

ROBERT (*irritably*): What did you say was the matter
with me?

RUTH: I wrote you had lung trouble.

ROBERT (*flying into a petty temper*): You *are* a fool!
How often have I explained to you that it's *pleurisy*
is the matter with me. You can't seem to get it in
your head that the pleura is outside the lungs, not
in them!

RUTH (*callously*): I only wrote what Doctor Smith
told me.

ROBERT (*angrily*): He's a damned ignoramus!

RUTH (*dully*): Makes no difference. I had to tell Andy
something, didn't I?

ROBERT (*after a pause, opening the other telegram*):
He sent this last evening. Let's see. (*He reads*)
"Leave for home on midnight train. Just received
your wire. Am bringing specialist to see Rob. Will
motor to farm from Port." (*He calculates*) What
time is it now?

RUTH: Round six, must be.

ROBERT: He ought to be here soon. I'm glad he's
bringing a doctor who knows something. A specialist will tell you in a second that there's nothing
the matter with my lungs.

RUTH (*stolidly*): You've been coughing an awful lot
lately.

ROBERT (*irritably*): What nonsense! For God's sake,
haven't you ever had a bad cold yourself? (RUTH

stares at the stove in silence. ROBERT *fidgets in his chair. There is a pause. Finally* ROBERT'S *eyes are fixed on the sleeping* MRS. ATKINS) Your mother is lucky to be able to sleep so soundly.

RUTH: Ma's tired. She's been sitting up with me most of the night.

ROBERT (*mockingly*): Is she waiting for Andy, too? (*There is a pause.* ROBERT *sighs*) I couldn't get to sleep to save my soul. I counted ten million sheep if I counted one. No use! I gave up trying finally and just laid there in the dark thinking. (*He pauses, then continues in a tone of tender sympathy*) I was thinking about you, Ruth—of how hard these last years must have been for you. (*Appealingly*) I'm sorry, Ruth.

RUTH (*in a dead voice*): I don't know. They're past now. They were hard on all of us.

ROBERT: Yes; on all of us but Andy. (*With a flash of sick jealousy*) Andy's made a big success of himself—the kind he wanted. (*Mockingly*) And now he's coming home to let us admire his greatness. (*Frowning—irritably*) What am I talking about? My brain must be sick, too. (*After a pause*) Yes, these years have been terrible for both of us. (*His voice is lowered to a trembling whisper*) Especially the last eight months since Mary—died. (*He forces back a sob with a convulsive shudder—then breaks out in a passionate agony*) Our last hope of happiness! I could curse God from the bottom of my soul—if there was a God! (*He is racked by a violent fit of coughing and hurriedly puts his handkerchief to his lips.*)

RUTH (*without looking at him*): Mary's better off—being dead.

ROBERT (*gloomily*): We'd all be better off for that matter. (*With a sudden exasperation*) You tell that mother of yours she's got to stop saying that Mary's

death was due to a weak constitution inherited from
me. (*On the verge of tears of weakness*) It's got to
stop, I tell you!

RUTH (*sharply*):   S-h-h! You'll wake her; and then
she'll nag at me—not you.

ROBERT (*coughs and lies back in his chair weakly—a
pause*):   It's all because your mother's down on me
for not begging Andy for help.

RUTH (*resentfully*):   You might have. He's got plenty.

ROBERT: How can *you* of all people think of taking
money from *him*?

RUTH (*dully*):   I don't see the harm. He's your own
brother.

ROBERT (*shrugging his shoulders*):   What's the use of
talking to you? Well, I couldn't. (*Proudly*) And I've
managed to keep things going, thank God. You
can't deny that without help I've succeeded in— (*He
breaks off with a bitter laugh*) My God, what am I
boasting of? Debts to this one and that, taxes, interest unpaid! I'm a fool! (*He lies back in his chair
closing his eyes for a moment, then speaks in a low
voice*) I'll be frank, Ruth. I've been an utter failure,
and I've dragged you with me. I couldn't blame you
in all justice—for hating me.

RUTH (*without feeling*):   I don't hate you. It's been
my fault too, I s'pose.

ROBERT: No. You couldn't help loving—Andy.

RUTH (*dully*):   I don't love anyone.

ROBERT (*waving her remark aside*):   You needn't
deny it. It doesn't matter. (*After a pause—with a
tender smile*) Do you know, Ruth, what I've been
dreaming back there in the dark? (*With a short
laugh*) I was planning our future when I get well.
(*He looks at her with appealing eyes as if afraid she
will sneer at him. Her expression does not change.
She stares at the stove. His voice takes on a note of
eagerness*) After all, why shouldn't we have a fu-

ture? We're young yet. If we can only shake off the curse of this farm! It's the farm that's ruined our lives, damn it! And now that Andy's coming back— I'm going to sink my foolish pride, Ruth! I'll borrow the money from him to give us a good start in the city. We'll go where people live instead of stagnating, and start all over again. (*Confidently*) I won't be the failure there that I've been here, Ruth. You won't need to be ashamed of me there. I'll prove to you the reading I've done can be put to some use. (*Vaguely*) I'll write, or something of that sort. I've always wanted to write. (*Pleadingly*) You'll want to do that, won't you, Ruth?

RUTH (*dully*):   There's Ma.

ROBERT: She can come with us.

RUTH: She wouldn't.

ROBERT (*angrily*):   So that's your answer! (*He trembles with violent passion. His voice is so strange that* RUTH *turns to look at him in alarm*) You're lying, Ruth! Your mother's just an excuse. You want to stay here. You think that because Andy's coming back that— (*He chokes and has an attack of coughing.*)

RUTH (*getting up—in a frightened voice*):   What's the matter? (*She goes to him*) I'll go with you, Rob. Stop that coughing for goodness' sake! It's awful bad for you. (*She soothes him in dull tones*) I'll go with you to the city—soon's you're well again. Honest I will, Rob, I promise! (ROB *lies back and closes his eyes. She stands looking down at him anxiously*) Do you feel better now?

ROBERT: Yes. (RUTH *goes back to her chair. After a pause he opens his eyes and sits up in his chair. His face is flushed and happy*) Then you *will* go, Ruth?

RUTH: Yes.

ROBERT (*excitedly*):   We'll make a new start, Ruth— just you and I. Life owes us some happiness after what we've been through. (*Vehemently*) It must! Otherwise our suffering would be meaningless— and that is unthinkable.

RUTH (*worried by his excitement*): Yes, yes, of course, Rob, but you mustn't—

ROBERT: Oh, don't be afraid. I feel completely well, really I do—now that I can hope again. Oh if you knew how glorious it feels to have something to look forward to! Can't you feel the thrill of it, too— the vision of a new life opening up after all the horrible years?

RUTH: Yes, yes, but do be—

ROBERT: Nonsense! I won't be careful. I'm getting back all my strength. (*He gets lightly to his feet*) See! I feel light as a feather. (*He walks to her chair and bends down to kiss her smilingly*) One kiss—the first in years, isn't it?—to greet the dawn of a new life together.

RUTH (*submitting to his kiss—worriedly*): Sit down, Rob, for goodness' sake!

ROBERT (*with tender obstinacy—stroking her hair*): I won't sit down. You're silly to worry. (*He rests one hand on the back of her chair*) Listen. All our suffering has been a test through which we had to pass to prove ourselves worthy of a finer realization. (*Exultingly*) And we did pass through it! It hasn't broken us! And now the dream is to come true! Don't you see?

RUTH (*looking at him with frightened eyes as if she thought he had gone mad*): Yes, Rob, I see; but won't you go back to bed now and rest?

ROBERT: No. I'm going to see the sun rise. It's an augury of good fortune. (*He goes quickly to the window in the rear left, and pushing the curtains aside, stands looking out. RUTH springs to her feet and comes quickly to the table, left, where she re-*

mains watching ROBERT *in a tense, expectant attitude. As he peers out his body seems gradually to
sag, to grow limp and tired. His voice is mournful
as he speaks*) No sun yet. It isn't time. All I can see
is the black rim of the damned hills outlined against
a creeping grayness. (*He turns around; letting the
curtains fall back, stretching a hand out to the wall
to support himself. His false strength of a moment
has evaporated leaving his face drawn and hollow-
eyed. He makes a pitiful attempt to smile*) That's
not a very happy augury, is it? But the sun'll come—
soon. (*He sways weakly.*)

RUTH (*hurrying to his side and supporting him*):
Please go to bed, won't you, Rob? You don't
want to be all wore out when the specialist comes,
do you?

ROBERT (*quickly*): No. That's right. He mustn't think
I'm sicker than I am. And I feel as if I could sleep
now— (*Cheerfully*) a good, sound, restful sleep.

RUTH (*helping him to the bedroom door*): That's
what you need most. (*They go inside. A moment
later she reappears calling back*) I'll shut this door
so's you'll be quiet. (*She closes the door and goes
quickly to her mother and shakes her by the shoulder*) Ma! Ma! Wake up!

MRS. ATKINS (*coming out of her sleep with a start*):
Glory be! What's the matter with you?

RUTH: It was Rob. He's just been talking to me out
here. I put him back to bed. (*Now that she is sure
her mother is awake her fear passes and she relapses
into dull indifference. She sits down in her chair and
stares at the stove—dully*) He acted—funny; and his
eyes looked so—so wild like.

MRS. ATKINS (*with asperity*): And is that all you
woke me out of a sound sleep for, and scared me
near out of my wits?

RUTH: I was afraid. He talked so crazy. I couldn't quiet him. I didn't want to be alone with him that way. Lord knows what he might do.

MRS. ATKINS (*scornfully*):   Humph! A help I'd be to you and me not able to move a step! Why didn't you run and get Jake?

RUTH (*dully*):   Jake isn't here. He quit last night. He hasn't been paid in three months.

MRS. ATKINS (*indignantly*):   I can't blame him. What decent person'd want to work on a place like this? (*With sudden exasperation*) Oh, I wish you'd never married that man!

RUTH (*wearily*):   You oughtn't to talk about him now when he's sick in his bed.

MRS. ATKINS (*working herself into a fit of rage*):   You know very well, Ruth Mayo, if it wasn't for me helpin' you on the sly out of my savin's, you'd both been in the poor house—and all 'count of his pig-headed pride in not lettin' Andy know the state thin's were in. A nice thin' for me to have to support him out of what I'd saved for my last days—and me an invalid with no one to look to!

RUTH: Andy'll pay you back, Ma. I can tell him so's Rob'll never know.

MRS. ATKINS (*with a snort*):   What'd Rob think you and him was livin' on, I'd like to know?

RUTH (*dully*):   He didn't think about it, I s'pose. (*After a slight pause*) He said he'd made up his mind to ask Andy for help when he comes. (*As a clock in the kitchen strikes six*) Six o'clock. Andy ought to get here directly.

MRS. ATKINS: D'you think this special doctor'll do Rob any good?

RUTH (*hopelessly*):   I don't know. (*The two women remain silent for a time staring dejectedly at the stove.*)

MRS. ATKINS (*shivering irritably*): For goodness' sake put some wood on that fire. I'm 'most freezin'!

RUTH (*pointing to the door in the rear*): Don't talk so loud. Let him sleep if he can. (*She gets wearily from the chair and puts a few pieces of wood in the stove*) This is the last of the wood. I don't know who'll cut more now that Jake's left. (*She sighs and walks to the window in the rear, left, pulls the curtains aside, and looks out*) It's getting gray out. (*She comes back to the stove*) Looks like it'd be a nice day. (*She stretches out her hands to warm them*) Must've been a heavy frost last night. We're paying for the spell of warm weather we've been having. (*The throbbing whine of a motor sounds from the distance outside.*)

MRS. ATKINS (*sharply*): S-h-h! Listen! Ain't that an auto I hear?

RUTH (*without interest*): Yes. It's Andy, I s'pose.

MRS. ATKINS (*with nervous irritation*): Don't sit there like a silly goose. Look at the state of this room! What'll this strange doctor think of us? Look at that lamp chimney all smoke! Gracious sakes, Ruth—

RUTH (*indifferently*): I've got a lamp all cleaned up in the kitchen.

MRS. ATKINS (*peremptorily*): Wheel me in there this minute. I don't want him to see me looking a sight. I'll lay down in the room the other side. You don't need me now and I'm dead for sleep. (RUTH *wheels her mother off right. The noise of the motor grows louder and finally ceases as the car stops on the road before the farmhouse.* RUTH *returns from the kitchen with a lighted lamp in her hand which she sets on the table beside the other. The sound of footsteps on the path is heard—then a sharp rap on the door.* RUTH *goes and opens it.* ANDREW *enters, followed by* DOCTOR FAWCETT *carrying a small black bag.* ANDREW *has changed greatly. His face seems to have grown highstrung, hardened by the look of decisiveness which comes from being constantly under a strain where judgments on the spur of the moment are compelled to be accurate. His eyes are keener and more alert. There is even a suggestion of ruthless cunning about them. At present, however, his expression is one of tense anxiety.* DOCTOR FAWCETT *is a short, dark, middle-aged man with a Vandyke beard. He wears glasses.*)

RUTH: Hello, Andy! I've been waiting—

ANDREW (*kissing her hastily*): I got here as soon as I could. (*He throws off his cap and heavy overcoat on the table, introducing* RUTH *and the* DOCTOR *as he does so. He is dressed in an expensive business suit and appears stouter*) My sister-in-law, Mrs. Mayo—Doctor Fawcett. (*They bow to each other silently.* ANDREW *casts a quick glance about the room*) Where's Rob?

RUTH (*pointing*): In there.

ANDREW: I'll take your coat and hat, Doctor. (*As he helps the* DOCTOR *with his things*) Is he very bad, Ruth?

RUTH (*dully*): He's been getting weaker.

ANDREW: Damn! This way, Doctor. Bring the lamp, Ruth. (*He goes into the bedroom, followed by the* DOCTOR *and* RUTH *carrying the clean lamp.* RUTH *reappears almost immediately closing the door behind her, and goes slowly to the outside door, which she opens, and stands in the doorway looking out. The sound of* ANDREW'S *and* ROBERT'S *voices comes from the bedroom. A moment later* ANDREW *reenters, closing the door softly. He comes forward and sinks down in the rocker on the right of table, leaning his head on his hand. His face is drawn in a shocked expression of great grief. He sighs heavily, staring mournfully in front of him.* RUTH *turns*

*and stands watching him. Then she shuts the door
and returns to her chair by the stove, turning it so
she can face him.*)

ANDREW (*glancing up quickly—in a harsh voice*):
How long has this been going on?

RUTH: You mean—how long has he been sick?

ANDREW (*shortly*): Of course! What else?

RUTH: It was last summer he had a bad spell first,
but he's been ailin' ever since Mary died—eight
months ago.

ANDREW (*harshly*): Why didn't you let me know—
cable me? Do you want him to die, all of you? I'm
damned if it doesn't look that way! (*His voice
breaking*) Poor old chap! To be sick in this out-of-
the-way hole without anyone to attend to him but
a country quack! It's a damned shame!

RUTH (*dully*): I wanted to send you word once, but
he only got mad when I told him. He was too proud
to ask anything, he said.

ANDREW: Proud? To ask *me*? (*He jumps to his feet
and paces nervously back and forth*) I can't understand the way you've acted. Didn't you see how sick
he was getting? Couldn't you realize—why, I nearly
dropped in my tracks when I saw him! He looks—
(*He shudders*) terrible! (*With fierce scorn*) I suppose
you're so used to the idea of his being delicate that
you took his sickness as a matter of course. God, if
I'd only known!

RUTH (*without emotion*): A letter takes some time to
get where you were—and we couldn't afford to
telegraph. We owed everyone already, and I couldn't
ask Ma. She'd been giving me money out of her sav-
ings till she hadn't much left. Don't say anything to
Rob about it. I never told him. He'd only be mad at me
if he knew. But I had to, because—God knows how
we'd have got on if I hadn't.

ANDREW: You mean to say— (*His eyes seem to*

*take in the poverty-stricken appearance of the room
for the first time*) You sent that telegram to me collect. Was it because— (RUTH *nods silently.* ANDREW
pounds on the table with his fist) Good God! And
all this time I've been—why I've had everything!
(*He sits down in his chair and pulls it close to*
RUTH'S *impulsively*) But—I can't get it through my
head. Why? Why? What has happened? How did it
ever come about? Tell me!

RUTH (*dully*):   There's nothing much to tell. Things
kept getting worse, that's all—and Rob didn't seem
to care. He never took any interest since way back
when your Ma died. After that he got men to take
charge, and they nearly all cheated him—he
couldn't tell—and left one after another. Then after
Mary died he didn't pay no heed to anything any
more—just stayed indoors and took to reading
books again. So I had to ask Ma if she wouldn't
help us some.

ANDREW (*surprised and horrified*):   Why, damn it,
this is frightful! Rob must be mad not to have let
me know. Too proud to ask help of *me*! What's the
matter with him in God's name? (*A sudden, horrible
suspicion entering his mind*) Ruth! Tell me the truth.
His mind hasn't gone back on him, has it?

RUTH (*dully*):   I don't know. Mary's dying broke him
up terrible—but he's used to her being gone by this
time, I s'pose.

ANDREW (*looking at her queerly*):   Do you mean to
say *you're* used to it?

RUTH (*in a dead tone*):   There's a time comes—when
you don't mind any more—anything.

ANDREW (*looks at her fixedly for a moment—with
great pity*):   I'm sorry, Ruth—if I seemed to blame
you. I didn't realize— The sight of Rob lying in bed
there, so gone to pieces—it made me furious at
everyone. Forgive me, Ruth.

RUTH: There's nothing to forgive. It doesn't matter.

ANDREW (*springing to his feet again and pacing up and down*): Thank God I came back before it was too late. This doctor will know exactly what to do. That's the first thing to think of. When Rob's on his feet again we can get the farm working on a sound basis once more. I'll see to that—before I leave.

RUTH: You're going away again?

ANDREW: I've got to.

RUTH: You wrote Rob you was coming back to stay this time.

ANDREW: I expected to—until I got to New York. Then I learned certain facts that make it necessary. (*With a short laugh*) To be candid, Ruth, I'm not the rich man you've probably been led to believe by my letters—not now. I was when I wrote them. I made money hand over fist as long as I stuck to legitimate trading; but I wasn't content with that. I wanted it to come easier, so like all the rest of the idiots, I tried speculation. Oh, I won all right! Several times I've been almost a millionaire—on paper—and then come down to earth again with a bump. Finally the strain was too much. I got disgusted with myself and made up my mind to get out and come home and forget it and really live again. (*He gives a harsh laugh*) And now comes the funny part. The day before the steamer sailed I saw what I thought was a chance to become a millionaire again. (*He snaps his fingers*) That easy! I plunged. Then, before things broke, I left—I was so confident I couldn't be wrong. But when I landed in New York—I wired you I had business to wind up, didn't I? Well, it was the business that wound me up! (*He smiles grimly, pacing up and down, his hands in his pockets.*)

RUTH (*dully*): You found—you'd lost everything?

ANDREW (*sitting down again*): Practically. (*He takes a cigar from his pocket, bites the end off, and lights it*) Oh, I don't mean I'm dead broke. I've saved ten thousand from the wreckage, maybe twenty. But that's a poor showing for five years' hard work. That's why I'll have to go back. (*Confidently*) I can make it up in a year or so down there—and I don't need but a shoestring to start with. (*A weary expression comes over his face and he sighs heavily*) I wish I didn't have to. I'm sick of it all.

RUTH: It's too bad—things seem to go wrong so.

ANDREW (*shaking off his depression—briskly*): They might be much worse. There's enough left to fix the farm O.K. before I go. I won't leave 'til Rob's on his feet again. In the meantime I'll make things fly around here. (*With satisfaction*) I need a rest, and the kind of rest I need is hard work in the open— just like I used to do in the old days. (*Stopping abruptly and lowering his voice cautiously*) Not a word to Rob about my losing money! Remember that, Ruth! You can see why. If he's grown so touchy he'd never accept a cent if he thought I was hard up; see?

RUTH: Yes, Andy. (*After a pause, during which AN-DREW puffs at his cigar abstractedly, his mind evidently busy with plans for the future, the bedroom door is opened and DR. FAWCETT enters, carrying a bag. He closes the door quietly behind him and comes forward, a grave expression on his face. AN-DREW springs out of his chair.*)

ANDREW: Ah, Doctor! (*He pushes a chair between his own and RUTH'S*) Won't you have a chair?

FAWCETT (*glancing at his watch*): I must catch the nine o'clock back to the city. It's imperative. I have only a moment. (*Sitting down and clearing his throat—in a perfunctory, impersonal voice*) The case of your brother, Mr. Mayo, is— (*He stops and glances at RUTH and says meaningly to ANDREW*) Perhaps it would be better if you and I—

RUTH (*with dogged resentment*): I know what you mean, Doctor. (*Dully*) Don't be afraid I can't stand it. I'm used to bearing trouble by this time; and I can guess what you've found out. (*She hesitates for a moment—then continues in a monotonous voice*) Rob's going to die.

ANDREW (*angrily*): Ruth!

FAWCETT (*raising his hand as if to command silence*): I am afraid my diagnosis of your brother's condition forces me to the same conclusion as Mrs. Mayo's.

ANDREW (*groaning*): But, Doctor, surely—

FAWCETT (*calmly*): Your brother hasn't long to live—perhaps a few days, perhaps only a few hours. It's a marvel that he's alive at this moment. My examination revealed that both of his lungs are terribly affected.

ANDREW (*brokenly*): Good God! (RUTH *keeps her eyes fixed on her lap in a trance-like stare.*)

FAWCETT: I am sorry I have to tell you this. If there was anything that could be done—

ANDREW: There isn't anything?

FAWCETT (*shaking his head*): It's too late. Six months ago there might have—

ANDREW (*in anguish*): But if we were to take him to the mountains—or to Arizona—or—

FAWCETT: That might have prolonged his life six months ago. (ANDREW *groans*) But now— (*He shrugs his shoulders significantly.*)

ANDREW (*appalled by a sudden thought*): Good heavens, you haven't told him this, have you, Doctor?

FAWCETT: No. I lied to him. I said a change of climate— (*He looks at his watch again nervously*) I must leave you. (*He gets up.*)

ANDREW (*getting to his feet—insistently*): But there must still be some chance—

FAWCETT (*as if he were reassuring a child*): There is always that last chance—the miracle. (*He puts on*

his hat and coat—bowing to RUTH) Good-by, Mrs.
Mayo.

RUTH (*without raising her eyes—dully*):   Good-by.

ANDREW (*mechanically*):   I'll walk to the car with
you, Doctor. (*They go out of the door.* RUTH *sits
motionlessly. The motor is heard starting and the
noise gradually recedes into the distance.* ANDREW
*re-enters and sits down in his chair, holding his head
in his hands*) Ruth! (*She lifts her eyes to his*) Hadn't
we better go in and see him? God! I'm afraid to! I
know he'll read it in my face. (*The bedroom door
is noiselessly opened and* ROBERT *appears in the
doorway. His cheeks are flushed with fever, and his
eyes appear unusually large and brilliant.* ANDREW
continues with a groan) It can't be, Ruth. It can't
be as hopeless as he said. There's always a fighting
chance. We'll take Rob to Arizona. He's got to get
well. There *must* be a chance!

ROBERT (*in a gentle tone*):   Why must there, Andy?
(RUTH *turns and stares at him with terrified eyes.*)

ANDREW (*whirling around*):   Rob! (*Scoldingly*) What
are you doing out of bed? (*He gets up and goes to
him*) Get right back now and obey the Doc, or
you're going to get a licking from me!

ROBERT (*ignoring these remarks*):   Help me over to
the chair, please, Andy.

ANDREW: Like hell I will! You're going right back to
bed, that's where you're going, and stay there! (*He
takes hold of* ROBERT'S *arm.*)

ROBERT (*mockingly*):   Stay there 'til I die, eh, Andy?
(*Coldly*) Don't behave like a child. I'm sick of lying
down. I'll be more rested sitting up. (*As* ANDREW
hesitates—violently) I swear I'll get out of bed every
time you put me there. You'll have to sit on my
chest, and that wouldn't help my health any. Come
on, Andy. Don't play the fool. I want to talk to you,

and I'm going to. (*With a grim smile*) A dying man has some rights, hasn't he?

ANDREW (*with a shudder*): Don't talk that way, for God's sake! I'll only let you sit down if you'll promise that. Remember. (*He helps* ROBERT *to the chair between his own and* RUTH'S) Easy now! There you are! Wait, and I'll get a pillow for you. (*He goes into the bedroom.* ROBERT *looks at* RUTH *who shrinks away from him in terror.* ROBERT *smiles bitterly.* ANDREW *comes back with the pillow which he places behind* ROBERT'S *back*) How's that?

ROBERT (*with an affectionate smile*): Fine! Thank you! (*As* ANDREW *sits down*) Listen, Andy. You've asked me not to talk—and I won't after I've made my position clear. (*Slowly*) In the first place I know I'm dying. (RUTH *bows her head and covers her face with her hands. She remains like this all during the scene between the two brothers.*)

ANDREW: Rob! That isn't so!

ROBERT (*wearily*): It *is* so! Don't lie to me. After Ruth put me to bed before you came, I saw it clearly for the first time. (*Bitterly*) I'd been making plans for our future—Ruth's and mine—so it came hard at first—the realization. Then when the doctor examined me, I knew—although he tried to lie about it. And then to make sure I listened at the door to what he told you. So don't mock me with fairy tales about Arizona, or any such rot as that. Because I'm dying is no reason you should treat me as an imbecile or a coward. Now that I'm sure what's happening I can say Kismet to it with all my heart. It was only the silly uncertainty that hurt. (*There is a pause.* ANDREW *looks around in impotent anguish, not knowing what to say.* ROBERT *regards him with an affectionate smile.*)

ANDREW (*finally blurts out*): It isn't foolish. You

have got a chance. If you heard all the Doctor said that ought to prove it to you.

ROBERT: Oh, you mean when he spoke of the miracle? (*Dryly*) I don't believe in miracles—in my case. Besides, I know more than any doctor on earth *could* know—because I *feel* what's coming. (*Dismissing the subject*) But we've agreed not to talk of it. Tell me about yourself, Andy. That's what I'm interested in. Your letters were too brief and far apart to be illuminating.

ANDREW: I meant to write oftener.

ROBERT (*with a faint trance of irony*): I judge from them you've accomplished all you set out to do five years ago?

ANDREW: That isn't much to boast of.

ROBERT (*surprised*): Have you really, honestly reached that conclusion?

ANDREW: Well, it doesn't seem to amount to much now.

ROBERT: But you're rich, aren't you?

ANDREW (*with a quick glance at* RUTH): Yes, I s'pose so.

ROBERT: I'm glad. You can do to the farm all I've undone. But what did you do down there? Tell me. You went in the grain business with that friend of yours?

ANDREW: Yes. After two years I had a share in it. I sold out last year. (*He is answering* ROBERT'S *questions with great reluctance.*)

ROBERT: And then?

ANDREW: I went in on my own.

ROBERT: Still in grain?

ANDREW: Yes.

ROBERT: What's the matter? You look as if I were accusing you of something.

ANDREW: I'm proud enough of the first four years.

It's after that I'm not boasting of. I took to specu-
lating.

ROBERT: In wheat?

ANDREW: Yes.

ROBERT: And you made money—gambling?

ANDREW: Yes.

ROBERT (*thoughtfully*): I've been wondering what
the great change was in you. (*After a pause*) You—
a farmer—to gamble in a wheat pit with scraps of
paper. There's a spiritual significance in that picture,
Andy. (*He smiles bitterly*) I'm a failure, and Ruth's
another—but we can both justly lay some of the
blame for our stumbling on God. But you're the
deepest-dyed failure of the three, Andy. You've
spent eight years running away from yourself. Do
you see what I mean? You used to be a creator when
you loved the farm. You and life were in harmoni-
ous partnership. And now— (*He stops as if seeking
vainly for words*) My brain is muddled. But part of
what I mean is that your gambling with the thing
you used to love to create proves how far astray—
So you'll be punished. You'll have to suffer to win
back— (*His voice grows weaker and he sighs wearily*) It's no use. I can't say it. (*He lies back and closes
his eyes, breathing pantingly.*)

ANDREW (*slowly*): I think I know what you're driving at, Rob—and it's true, I guess. (ROBERT *smiles
gratefully and stretches out his hand, which* AN-
DREW *takes in his.*)

ROBERT: I want you to promise me to do one thing,
Andy, after—

ANDREW: I'll promise anything, as God is my Judge!

ROBERT: Remember, Andy, Ruth has suffered double
her share. (*His voice faltering with weakness*) Only
through contact with suffering, Andy, will you—
awaken. Listen. You must marry Ruth—afterwards.

RUTH (*with a cry*): Rob! (ROBERT *lies back, his eyes closed, gasping heavily for breath.*)

ANDREW (*making signs to her to humor him—gently*): You're tired out, Rob. You better lie down and rest a while, don't you think? We can talk later on.

ROBERT (*with a mocking smile*): Later on! You always were an optimist, Andy! (*He sighs with exhaustion*) Yes, I'll go and rest a while. (*As* ANDREW *comes to help him*) It must be near sunrise, isn't it?

ANDREW: It's after six.

ROBERT (*as* ANDREW *helps him into the bedroom*): Shut the door, Andy. I want to be alone. (ANDREW *reappears and shuts the door softly. He comes and sits down on his chair again, supporting his head on his hands. His face drawn with the intensity of his dry-eyed anguish.*)

RUTH (*glancing at him—fearfully*): He's out of his mind now, isn't he?

ANDREW: He may be a little delirious. The fever would do that. (*With impotent rage*) God, what a shame! And there's nothing we can do but sit and— wait! (*He springs from his chair and walks to the stove.*)

RUTH (*dully*): He was talking—wild—like he used to—only this time it sounded—unnatural, don't you think?

ANDREW: I don't know. The things he said to me had truth in them—even if he did talk them way up in the air, like he always sees things. Still— (*He glances down at* RUTH *keenly*) Why do you suppose he wanted us to promise we'd— (*Confusedly*) You know what he said.

RUTH (*dully*): His mind was wandering, I s'pose.

ANDREW (*with conviction*): No—there was something back of it.

RUTH: He wanted to make sure I'd be all right—after he'd gone, I expect.

ANDREW: No, it wasn't that. He knows very well I'd naturally look after you without—anything like that.

RUTH: He might be thinking of—something happened five years back, the time you came home from the trip.

ANDREW: What happened? What do you mean?

RUTH (*dully*): We had a fight.

ANDREW: A fight? What has that to do with me?

RUTH: It was about you—in a way.

ANDREW (*amazed*): About *me*?

RUTH: Yes, mostly. You see I'd found out I'd made a mistake about Rob soon after we were married—when it was too late.

ANDREW: Mistake? (*Slowly*) You mean—you found out you didn't love Rob?

RUTH: Yes.

ANDREW: Good God!

RUTH: And then I thought that when Mary came it'd be different, and I'd love him; but it didn't happen that way. And I couldn't bear with his blundering and book-reading—and I grew to hate him, almost.

ANDREW: Ruth!

RUTH: I couldn't help it. No woman could. It had to be because I loved someone else, I'd found out. (*She sighs wearily*) It can't do no harm to tell you now—when it's all past and gone—and dead. *You* were the one I really loved—only I didn't come to the knowledge of it 'til too late.

ANDREW (*stunned*): Ruth! Do you know what you're saying?

RUTH: It was true—then. (*With sudden fierceness*) How could I help it? No woman could.

ANDREW: Then—you loved me—that time I came home?

RUTH (*doggedly*): I'd known your real reason for

leaving home the first time—everybody knew it—
and for three years I'd been thinking—

ANDREW: That I loved you?

RUTH: Yes. Then that day on the hill you laughed
about what a fool you'd been for loving me once—
and I knew it was all over.

ANDREW: Good God, but I never thought— (*He
stops, shuddering at his remembrance*) And did
Rob—

RUTH: That was what I'd started to tell. We'd had a
fight just before you came and I got crazy mad—
and I told him all I've told you.

ANDREW (*gaping at her speechlessly for a moment*):
You told Rob—you loved me?

RUTH: Yes.

ANDREW (*shrinking away from her in horror*):
You—you—you mad fool, you! How could you do
such a thing?

RUTH: I couldn't help it. I'd got to the end of bearing
things—without talking.

ANDREW: Then Rob must have known every moment I stayed here! And yet he never said or
showed—God, how he must have suffered! Didn't
you know how much he loved you?

RUTH (*dully*): Yes. I knew he liked me.

ANDREW: Liked you! What kind of a woman are
you? Couldn't you have kept silent? Did you have
to torture him? No wonder he's dying! And you've
lived together for five years with this between you?

RUTH: We've lived in the same house.

ANDREW: Does he still think—

RUTH: I don't know. We've never spoke a word
about it since that day. Maybe, from the way he
went on, he s'poses I care for you yet.

ANDREW: But you don't. It's outrageous. It's stupid!
You don't love me!

RUTH (*slowly*): I wouldn't know how to feel love, even if I tried, any more.

ANDREW (*brutally*): And I don't love you, that's sure! (*He sinks into his chair, his head between his hands*) It's damnable such a thing should be between Rob and me. Why, I love Rob better'n anybody in the world and always did. There isn't a thing on God's green earth I wouldn't have done to keep trouble away from him. And I have to be the very one—it's damnable! How am I going to face him again? What can I say to him now? (*He groans with anguished rage. After a pause*) He asked me to promise—what am I going to do?

RUTH: You can promise—so's it'll ease his mind—and not mean anything.

ANDREW: What? Lie to him now—when he's dying? (*Determinedly*) No! It's *you* who'll have to do the lying, since it must be done. You've got a chance now to undo some of all the suffering you've brought on Rob. Go in to him! Tell him you never loved me—it was all a mistake. Tell him you only said so because you were mad and didn't know what you were saying! Tell him something, anything, that'll bring him peace!

RUTH (*dully*): He wouldn't believe me.

ANDREW (*furiously*): You've got to make him believe you, do you hear? You've got to—now—hurry—you never know when it may be too late. (*As she hesitates—imploringly*) For God's sake, Ruth! Don't you see you owe it to him? You'll never forgive yourself if you don't.

RUTH (*dully*): I'll go. (*She gets wearily to her feet and walks slowly toward the bedroom*) But it won't do any good. (ANDREW'S *eyes are fixed on her anxiously. She opens the door and steps inside the room. She remains standing there for a minute.*

Then she calls in a frightened voice) Rob! Where are you? (*Then she hurries back, trembling with fright*) Andy! Andy! He's gone!

ANDREW (*misunderstanding her—his face pale with dread*): He's not—

RUTH (*interrupting him—hysterically*): He's gone! The bed's empty. The window's wide open. He must have crawled out into the yard!

ANDREW (*springing to his feet. He rushes into the bedroom and returns immediately with an expression of alarmed amazement on his face*): Come! He can't have gone far! (*Grabbing his hat he takes* RUTH'S *arm and shoves her toward the door*) Come on! (*Opening the door*) Let's hope to God— (*The door closes behind them, cutting off his words as the curtain falls.*)

Act Three

Scene 2

Same as Act One, Scene 1—A section of country high-way. The sky to the east is already alight with bright color and a thin, quivering line of flame is spreading slowly along the horizon rim of the dark hills. The roadside, however, is still steeped in the grayness of the dawn, shadowy and vague. The field in the fore-ground has a wild uncultivated appearance as if it had been allowed to remain fallow the preceding summer. Parts of the snake-fence in the rear have been broken down. The apple tree is leafless and seems dead.

ROBERT staggers weakly in from the left. He stum-bles into the ditch and lies there for a moment; then crawls with a great effort to the top of the bank where he can see the sun rise, and collapses weakly. RUTH and ANDREW come hurriedly along the road from the left.

ANDREW (*stopping and looking about him*): There he is! I knew it! I knew we'd find him here.

ROBERT (*trying to raise himself to a sitting position as they hasten to his side—with a wan smile*): I thought I'd given you the slip.

ANDREW (*with kindly bullying*): Well you didn't, you old scoundrel, and we're going to take you right back where you belong—in bed. (*He makes a mo-tion to lift ROBERT.*)

105

ROBERT: Don't, Andy. Don't, I tell you!

ANDREW: You're in pain?

ROBERT (*simply*): No. I'm dying. (*He falls back weakly.* RUTH *sinks down beside him with a sob and pillows his head on her lap.* ANDREW *stands looking down at him helplessly.* ROBERT *moves his head restlessly on* RUTH'S *lap*) I couldn't stand it back there in the room. It seemed as if all my life—I'd been cooped in a room. So I thought I'd try to end as I might have—if I'd had the courage—alone—in a ditch by the open road—watching the sun rise.

ANDREW: Rob! Don't talk. You're wasting your strength. Rest a while and then we'll carry you—

ROBERT: Still hoping, Andy? Don't. I know. (*There is a pause during which he breathes heavily, straining his eyes toward the horizon*) The sun comes so slowly. (*With an ironical smile*) The doctor told me to go to the far-off places—and I'd be cured. He was right. That was always the cure for me. It's too late—for this life—but— (*He has a fit of coughing which racks his body.*)

ANDREW (*with a hoarse sob*):   Rob! (*He clenches his fists in an impotent rage against Fate*) God! God! (RUTH *sobs brokenly and wipes* ROBERT'S *lips with her handkerchief.*)

ROBERT (*in a voice which is suddenly ringing with the happiness of hope*):   You mustn't feel sorry for me. Don't you see I'm happy at last—free—free!—freed from the farm—free to wander on and on—eternally! (*He raises himself on his elbow, his face radiant, and points to the horizon*) Look! Isn't it beautiful beyond the hills? I can hear the old voices calling me to come— (*Exultantly*) And this time I'm going! It isn't the end. It's a free beginning—the start of my voyage! I've won to my trip—the right of release—beyond the horizon! Oh, you ought to be glad—glad—for my sake! (*He collapses weakly*)

Andy! (ANDREW *bends down to him*) Remember
Ruth—

ANDREW: I'll take care of her, I swear to you, Rob!

ROBERT: Ruth has suffered—remember, Andy—only
through sacrifice—the secret beyond there— (*He
suddenly raises himself with his last remaining
strength and points to the horizon where the edge
of the sun's disc is rising from the rim of the hills*)
The sun! (*He remains with his eyes fixed on it for
a moment. A rattling noise throbs from his throat.
He mumbles*) Remember! (*And falls back and is
still.* RUTH *gives a cry of horror and springs to her
feet, shuddering, her hands over her eyes.* ANDREW
*bends on one knee beside the body, placing a hand
over* ROBERT'S *heart, then he kisses his brother rev-
erentially on the forehead and stands up.*)

ANDREW (*facing* RUTH, *the body between them—in a
dead voice*):   He's dead. (*With a sudden burst of
fury*) God damn you, you never told him!

RUTH (*piteously*):   He was so happy without my lying
to him.

ANDREW (*pointing to the body—trembling with the
violence of his rage*):   This is your doing, you damn
woman, you coward, you murderess!

RUTH (*sobbing*):   Don't, Andy! I couldn't help it—
and he knew how I'd suffered, too. He told you—
to remember.

ANDREW (*stares at her for a moment, his rage ebbing
away, an expression of deep pity gradually coming
over his face. Then he glances down at his brother
and speaks brokenly in a compassionate voice*):
Forgive me, Ruth—for his sake—and I'll remember— (RUTH *lets her hands fall from her face and
looks at him uncomprehendingly. He lifts his eyes
to hers and forces out falteringly*) I—you—we've
both made a mess of things! We must try to help
each other—and—in time—we'll come to know

what's right— (*Desperately*) And perhaps we—
(*But* RUTH, *if she is aware of his words, gives no
sign. She remains silent, gazing at him dully with
the sad humility of exhaustion, her mind already
sinking back into that spent calm beyond the further
troubling of any hope.*)

Curtain

The Emperor Jones

Characters

BRUTUS JONES, *Emperor*
HENRY SMITHERS, *A Cockney Trader*
AN OLD NATIVE WOMAN
LEM, *A Native Chief*
SOLDIERS, *Adherents of Lem*
The Little Formless Fears; Jeff; The Negro Convicts;
The Prison Guard; The Planters; The Auctioneer;
The Slaves; The Congo Witch-Doctor; The Crocodile
God

The action of the play takes place on an island in the West Indies as yet not self-determined by white Marines. The form of native government is, for the time being, an empire.

Scene One

The audience chamber in the palace of the Emperor—
a spacious, high-ceilinged room with bare, white-
washed walls. The floor is of white tiles. In the rear,
to the left of center, a wide archway giving out on a
portico with white pillars. The palace is evidently sit-
uated on high ground, for beyond the portico nothing
can be seen but a vista of distant hills, their summits
crowned with thick groves of palm trees. In the right
wall, center, a smaller arched doorway leading to the
living quarters of the palace. The room is bare of fur-
niture with the exception of one huge chair made of
uncut wood which stands at center, its back to rear.
This is very apparently the Emperor's throne. It is
painted a dazzling, eye-smiting scarlet. There is a brilliant orange cushion on the seat and another smaller
one is placed on the floor to serve as a footstool. Strips
of matting, dyed scarlet, lead from the foot of the
throne to the two entrances.

It is late afternoon but the sunlight still blazes yel-
lowly beyond the portico and there is an oppressive
burden of exhausting heat in the air.

As the curtain rises, a native Negro woman sneaks
in cautiously from the entrance on the right. She is
very old, dressed in cheap calico, bare-footed, a red
bandana handkerchief covering all but a few stray
wisps of white hair. A bundle bound in colored cloth
is carried over her shoulder on the end of a stick. She
hesitates beside the doorway, peering back as if in ex-

113

treme dread of being discovered. Then she begins to glide noiselessly a step at a time, toward the doorway in the rear. At this moment, SMITHERS *appears beneath the portico.*

SMITHERS *is a tall, stoop-shouldered man about forty. His bald head, perched on a long neck with an enormous Adam's apple, looks like an egg. The tropics have tanned his naturally pasty face with its small, sharp features to a sickly yellow, and native rum has painted his pointed nose to a startling red. His little, washy-blue eyes are red-rimmed and dart about him like a ferret's. His expression is one of unscrupulous meanness, cowardly and dangerous. He is dressed in a worn riding suit of dirty white drill, puttees, spurs, and wears a white cork helmet. A cartridge belt with an automatic revolver is around his waist. He carries a riding whip in his hand. He sees the woman and stops to watch her suspiciously. Then, making up his mind, he steps quickly on tiptoe into the room. The woman, looking back over her shoulder continually, does not see him until it is too late. When she does* SMITHERS *springs forward and grabs her firmly by the shoulder. She struggles to get away, fiercely but silently.*

SMITHERS [*Tightening his grasp—roughly*]: Easy! None o' that, me birdie. You can't wriggle out now. I got me 'ooks on yer.
WOMAN [*Seeing the uselessness of struggling, gives way to frantic terror, and sinks to the ground, embracing his knees supplicatingly*]: No tell him! No tell him, Mister!
SMITHERS [*With great curiosity*]: Tell 'im? [*Then scornfully*] Oh, you mean 'is bloomin' Majesty. What's the gaime, any 'ow? What are you sneakin' away for? Been stealin' a bit, I s'pose. [*He taps her bundle with his riding whip significantly.*]

WOMAN [*Shaking her head vehemently*]: No, me no steal.

SMITHERS: Bloody liar! But tell me what's up. There's somethin' funny goin' on. I smelled it in the air first thing I got up this mornin'. You blacks are up to some devilment. This palace of 'is is like a bleedin' tomb. Where's all the 'ands? [*The woman keeps sullenly silent.* SMITHERS *raises his whip threateningly.*] Ow, yer won't, won't yer? I'll show yer what's what.

WOMAN [*Coweringly*]: I tell, Mister. You no hit. They go—all go. [*She makes a sweeping gesture toward the hills in the distance.*]

SMITHERS: Run away—to the 'ills?

WOMAN: Yes, Mister. Him Emperor—Great Father. [*She touches her forehead to the floor with a quick mechanical jerk.*] Him sleep after eat. Then they go—all go. Me old woman. Me left only. Now me go too.

SMITHERS [*His astonishment giving way to an immense, mean satisfaction*]: Ow! So that's the ticket! Well, I know bloody well wot's in the air— when they runs orf to the 'ills. The tom-tom 'll be thumping out there bloomin' soon. [*With extreme vindictiveness*] And I'm bloody glad of it, for one! Serve 'im right! Puttin' on airs, the stinkin' nigger! 'Is Majesty! Gawd blimey! I only 'opes I'm there when they takes 'im out to shoot 'im. [*Suddenly*] 'E's still 'ere all right, ain't 'e?

WOMAN: Yes. Him sleep.

SMITHERS: 'E's bound to find out soon as 'e wakes up. 'E's cunnin' enough to know when 'is time's come. [*He goes to the doorway on right and whistles shrilly with his fingers in his mouth. The old woman springs to her feet and runs out of the doorway, rear.* SMITHERS *goes after her, reaching for his revolver.*] Stop or I'll shoot! [*Then stopping—indif-*

ferently] Pop orf then, if yer like, yer black cow. [*He stands in the doorway, looking after her.*]

[JONES *enters from the right. He is a tall, powerfully-built, full-blooded Negro of middle age. His features are typically negroid, yet there is something decidedly distinctive about his face—an underlying strength of will, a hardy, self-reliant confidence in himself that inspires respect. His eyes are alive with a keen, cunning intelligence. In manner he is shrewd, suspicious, evasive. He wears a light blue uniform coat, sprayed with brass buttons, heavy gold chevrons on his shoulders, gold braid on the collar, cuffs, etc. His pants are bright red with a light blue stripe down the side. Patent-leather laced boots with brass spurs, and a belt with a long-barreled, pearl-handled revolver in a holster complete his make up. Yet there is something not altogether ridiculous about his grandeur. He has a way of carrying it off.*]

JONES [*Not seeing anyone—greatly irritated and blinking sleepily—shouts*]: Who dare whistle dat way in my palace? Who dare wake up de Emperor? I'll git de hide fravled off some o' you niggers sho'!

SMITHERS [*Showing himself—in a manner half-afraid and half-defiant*]: It was me whistled to yer. [*As* JONES *frowns angrily*] I got news for yer.

JONES [*Putting on his suavest manner, which fails to cover up his contempt for the white man*]: Oh, it's you, Mister Smithers. [*He sits down on his throne with easy dignity*] What news you got to tell me?

SMITHERS [*Coming close to enjoy his discomfiture*]: Don't yer notice nothin' funny today?

JONES [*Coldly*]: Funny? No, I ain't perceived nothin' of de kind!

SMITHERS: Then yer ain't so foxy as I thought yer

was. Where's all your court? [*Sarcastically*] The
Generals and the Cabinet Ministers and all?

JONES [*Imperturbably*]: Where dey mostly runs de
minute I close my eyes—drinkin' rum and talkin'
big down in de town. [*Sarcastically*] How come you
don't know dat? Ain't you sousin' with 'em most
every day?

SMITHERS [*Stung but pretending indifference—with a
wink*]: That's part of the day's work. I got ter—
ain't I—in my business?

JONES [*Contemptuously*]: Yo' business!

SMITHERS [*Imprudently enraged*]: Gawd blimey, you
was glad enough for me ter take yer in on it when
you landed here first. You didn' 'ave no 'igh and
mighty airs in them days!

JONES [*His hand going to his revolver like a flash—
menacingly*]: Talk polite, white man! Talk polite,
you heah me! I'm boss heah now, is you fergettin'?
[*The Cockney seems about to challenge this last
statement with the facts but something in the other's
eyes holds and cows him.*]

SMITHERS [*In a cowardly whine*]: No 'arm meant,
old top.

JONES [*Condescendingly*]: I accept yo' apology. [*Lets
his hand fall from his revolver*] No use'n you rakin'
up ole times. What I was den is one thing. What I
is now 's another. You didn't let me in on yo'
crooked work out o' no kind feelin's dat time. I
done de dirty work fo' you—and most o' de brain
work, too, fo' dat matter—and I was wu'th money
to you, dat's de reason.

SMITHERS: Well, blimey, I give yer a start, didn't I—
when no one else would. I wasn't afraid to 'ire yer
like the rest was—'count of the story about your
breakin' jail back in the States.

JONES: No, you didn't have no s'cuse to look down
on me fo' dat. You been in jail you'self more'n once.

SMITHERS [*Furiously*]:   It's a lie! [*Then trying to pass it off by an attempt at scorn*] Garn! Who told yer that fairy tale?

JONES: Dey's some tings I ain't got to be tole. I kin see 'em in folk's eyes. [*Then after a pause—meditatively*] Yes, you sho' give me a start. And it didn't take long from dat time to git dese fool, woods' niggers right where I wanted dem. [*With pride*] From stowaway to Emperor in two years! Dat's goin' some!

SMITHERS [*With curiosity*]:   And I bet you got yer pile o' money 'id safe some place.

JONES [*With satisfaction*]:   I sho' has! And it's in a foreign bank where no pusson don't ever git it out but me no matter what come. You didn't s'pose I was holdin' down dis Emperor job for de glory in it, did you? Sho'! De fuss and glory part of it, dat's only to turn de heads o' de low-flung, bush niggers dat's here. Dey wants de big circus show for deir money. I gives it to 'em an' I gits de money. [*With a grin*] De long green, dat's me every time! [*Then rebukingly*] But you ain't got no kick agin me, Smithers. I'se paid you back all you done for me many times. Ain't I pertected you and winked at all de crooked tradin' you been doin' right out in de broad day? Sho' I has—and me makin' laws to stop it at de same time! [*He chuckles.*]

SMITHERS [*Grinning*]:   But, meanin' no 'arm, you been grabbin' right and left yourself, ain't yer? Look at the taxes you've put on 'em! Blimey! You've squeezed 'em dry!

JONES [*Chuckling*]:   No, dey ain't *all* dry yet. I'se still heah, ain't I?

SMITHERS [*Smiling at his secret thought*]:   They're dry right now, you'll find out. [*Changing the subject abruptly*] And as for me breakin' laws, you've broke 'em all yerself just as fast as yer made 'em.

JONES: Ain't I de Emperor? De laws don't go for him. [*Judicially*] You heah what I tells you, Smithers. Dere's little stealin' like you does, and dere's big stealin' like I does. For de little stealin' dey gits you in jail soon or late. For de big stealin' dey makes you Emperor and puts you in de Hall o' Fame when you croaks. [*Reminiscently*] If dey's one thing I learns in ten years on de Pullman ca's listenin' to de white quality talk, it's dat same fact. And when I gits a chance to use it I winds up Emperor in two years.

SMITHERS [*Unable to repress the genuine admiration of the small fry for the large*]: Yes, yer turned the bleedin' trick, all right. Blimey, I never seen a bloke 'as 'ad the bloomin' luck you 'as.

JONES [*Severely*]: Luck? What you mean—luck?

SMITHERS: I suppose you'll say as that swank about the silver bullet ain't luck—and that was what first got the fool blacks on yer side the time of the revolution, wasn't it?

JONES [*With a laugh*]: Oh, dat silver bullet! Sho' was luck! But I makes dat luck, you heah? I loads de dice! Yessuh! When dat murderin' nigger ole Lem hired to kill me takes aim ten feet away and his gun misses fire and I shoots him dead, what you heah me say?

SMITHERS: You said yer'd got a charm so's no lead bullet'd kill yer. You was so strong only a silver bullet could kill yer, you told 'em. Blimey, wasn't that swank for yer—and plain, fat-'eaded luck?

JONES [*Proudly*]: I got brains and I uses 'em quick. Dat ain't luck.

SMITHERS: Yer know they wasn't 'ardly liable to get no silver bullets. And it was luck 'e didn't 'it you that time.

JONES [*Laughing*]: And dere all dem fool, bush niggers was kneelin' down and bumpin' deir heads on

de ground like I was a miracle out o' de Bible. Oh
Lawd, from dat time on I had dem all eatin' out of
my hand. I cracks de whip and dey jumps through.

SMITHERS [*With a sniff*]: Yankee bluff done it.

JONES: Ain't a man's talkin' big what makes him
big—long as he makes folks believe it? Sho', I talks
large when I ain't got nothin' to back it up, but I
ain't talkin' wild just de same. I knows I kin fool
'em—I *knows* it—and dat's backin' enough fo' my
game. And ain't I got to learn deir lingo and teach
some of dem English befo' I kin to talk to 'em? Ain't
dat wuk? You ain't never learned ary word er it,
Smithers, in de ten years you been heah, dough yo'
knows it's money in yo' pocket tradin' wid 'em if
you does. But you'se too shiftless to take de trouble.

SMITHERS [*Flushing*]: Never mind about me. What's
this I've 'eard about yer really 'avin' a silver bullet
moulded for yourself?

JONES: It's playin' out my bluff. I has de silver bullet
moulded and I tells 'em when de time comes I kills
myself wid it. I tells 'em dat's 'cause I'm de on'y
man in de world big enough to git me. No use'n
deir tryin'. And dey falls down and bumps deir
heads. [*He laughs.*] I does dat so's I kin take a walk
in peace widout no jealous nigger gunnin' at me
from behind de trees.

SMITHERS [*Astonished*]: Then you 'ad it made—
'onest?

JONES: Sho' did. Heah she be. [*He takes out his revolver, breaks it, and takes the silver bullet out of
one chamber.*] Five lead an' dis silver baby at de
last. Don't she shine pretty? [*He holds it in his hand,
looking at it admiringly, as if strangely fascinated.*]

SMITHERS: Let me see. [*Reaches out his hand for it*]

JONES [*Harshly*]: Keep yo' hands whar dey b'long,
white man. [*He replaces it in the chamber and puts
the revolver back on his hip.*]

SMITHERS [*Snarling*]: Gawd blimey! Think I'm a bleedin' thief, you would.

JONES: No, 'tain't dat. I knows you'se scared to steal from me. On'y I ain't 'lowin' nary body to touch dis baby. She's my rabbit's foot.

SMITHERS [*Sneering*]: A bloomin' charm, wot? [*Venomously*] Well, you'll need all the bloody charms you 'as before long, s' 'elp me!

JONES [*Judicially*]: Oh, I'se good for six months yit 'fore dey gits sick o' my game. Den, when I sees trouble comin', I makes my getaway.

SMITHERS: Ho! You got it all planned, ain't yer?

JONES: I ain't no fool. I knows dis Emperor's time is sho't. Dat why I make hay when de sun shine. Was you thinkin' I'se aimin' to hold down dis job for life? No, suh! What good is gittin' money if you stays back in dis raggedy country? I wants action when I spends. And when I sees dese niggers gittin' up deir nerve to tu'n me out, and I'se got all de money in sight, I resigns on de spot and beats it quick.

SMITHERS: Where to?

JONES: None o' yo' business.

SMITHERS: Not back to the bloody States, I'll lay my oath.

JONES [*Suspiciously*]: Why don't I? [*Then with an easy laugh*] You mean 'count of dat story 'bout me breakin' from jail back dere? Dat's all talk.

SMITHERS [*Skeptically*]: Ho, yes!

JONES [*Sharply*]: You ain't 'sinuatin' I'se a liar, is you?

SMITHERS [*Hastily*]: No, Gawd strike me! I was only thinkin' o' the bloody lies you told the blacks 'ere about killin' white men in the States.

JONES [*Angered*]: How come dey're lies?

SMITHERS: You'd 'ave been in jail if you 'ad, wouldn't yer then? [*With venom*] And from what

I've 'eard, it ain't 'ealthy for a black to kill a white man in the States. They burns 'em in oil, don't they?

JONES [*With cool deadliness*]: You mean lynchin' 'd scare me? Well, I tells you, Smithers, maybe I does kill one white man back dere. Maybe I does. And maybe I kills another right heah 'fore long if he don't look out.

SMITHERS [*Trying to force a laugh*]: I was on'y spoofin' yer. Can't yer take a joke? And you was just sayin' you'd never been in jail.

JONES [*In the same tone—slightly boastful*]: Maybe I goes to jail dere for gettin' in an argument wid razors ovah a crap game. Maybe I gits twenty years when dat colored man die. Maybe I gits in 'nother argument wid de prison guard was overseer ovah us when we're wukin' de roads. Maybe he hits me wid a whip and I splits his head wid a shovel and runs away and files de chain off my leg and gits away safe. Maybe I does all dat an' maybe I don't. It's a story I tells you so's you knows I'se de kind of man dat if you evah repeats one word of it, I ends yo' stealin' on dis yearth mighty damn quick!

SMITHERS [*Terrified*]: Think I'd peach on yer? Not me! Ain't I always been yer friend?

JONES [*Suddenly relaxing*]: Sho' you has—and you better be.

SMITHERS [*Recovering his composure—and with it his malice*]: And just to show yer I'm yer friend, I'll tell yer that bit o' news I was goin' to.

JONES: Go ahead! Shoot de piece. Must be bad news from de happy way you look.

SMITHERS [*Warningly*]: Maybe it's gettin' time for you to resign—with that bloomin' silver bullet, wot? [*He finishes with a mocking grin.*]

JONES [*Puzzled*]: What's dat you say? Talk plain.

SMITHERS: Ain't noticed any of the guards or servants about the place today, I 'aven't.

JONES [*Carelessly*]: Dey're all out in de garden sleepin' under de trees. When I sleeps, dey sneaks a sleep, too, and I pretends I never suspicions it. All I got to do is to ring de bell and dey come flyin', makin' a bluff dey was wukin' all de time.

SMITHERS [*In the same mocking tone*]: Ring the bell now an' you'll bloody well see what I means.

JONES [*Startled to alertness, but preserving the same careless tone*]: Sho' I rings. [*He reaches below the throne and pulls out a big, common dinner bell which is painted the same vivid scarlet as the throne. He rings this vigorously—then stops to listen. Then he goes to both doors, rings again, and looks out.*]

SMITHERS [*Watching him with malicious satisfaction, after a pause—mockingly*]: The bloody ship is sinkin' an' the bleedin' rats 'as slung their 'ooks.

JONES [*In a sudden fit of anger flings the bell clattering into a corner*]: Low-flung, woods' niggers! [*Then catching Smithers' eye on him, he controls himself and suddenly bursts into a low chuckling laugh.*] Reckon I overplays my hand dis once! A man can't take de pot on a bob-tailed flush all de time. Was I sayin' I'd sit in six months mo'? Well, I'se changed my mind den, I cashes in and resigns de job of Emperor right dis minute.

SMITHERS [*With real admiration*]: Blimey, but you're a cool bird, and no mistake.

JONES: No use'n fussin'. When I knows de game's up I kisses it good-bye widout no long waits. Dey've all run off to de hills, ain't dey?

SMITHERS: Yes—every bleedin' man jack of 'em.

JONES: Den de revolution is at de post. And de Emperor better git his feet smokin' up de trail. [*He starts for the door in rear.*]

SMITHERS: Goin' out to look for your 'orse? Yer won't find any. They steals the 'orses first thing.

Mine was gone when I went for 'im this mornin'.
That's wot first give me a suspicion of wot was up.

JONES [*Alarmed for a second, scratches his head, then
philosophically*]: Well, den I hoofs it. Feet, do yo'
duty! [*He pulls out a gold watch and looks at it.*]
Three-thuty. Sundown's at six-thuty or dere-abouts.
[*Puts his watch back—with cool confidence*] I got
plenty o' time to make it easy.

SMITHERS: Don't be so bloomin' sure of it. They'll be
after you 'ot and 'eavy. Ole Lem is at the bottom
o' this business an' 'e 'ates you like 'ell. 'E'd rather
do for you than eat 'is dinner,'e would!

JONES [*Scornfully*]: Dat fool no-count nigger! Does
you think I'se scared o' him? I stands him on his
thick head mor'n once befo' dis, and I does it again
if he come in my way . . . [*Fiercely*] And dis time I
leave him a dead nigger fo' sho'!

SMITHERS: You'll 'ave to cut through the big forest—
an' these blacks 'ere can sniff and follow a trail in
the dark like 'ounds. You'd 'ave to 'ustle to get
through that forest in twelve hours even if you knew
all the bloomin' trails like a native.

JONES [*With indignant scorn*]: Look-a-heah, white
man! Does you think I'se a natural bo'n fool? Give
me credit fo' havin' some sense, fo' Lawd's sake!
Don't you s'pose I'se looked ahead and made sho'
of all de chances? I'se gone out in dat big forest,
pretendin' to hunt, so many times dat I knows it
high an' low like a book. I could go through on dem
trails wid my eyes shut. [*With great contempt*]
Think dese ign'rent bush niggers dat ain't got brains
enuff to know deir own names even can catch Brutus Jones? Huh, I s'pects not! Not on yo' life! Why,
man, de white men went after me wid bloodhounds
where I come from an I jes' laughs at 'em. It's a
shame to fool dese black trash around heah, dey're

so easy. You watch me, man! I'll make dem look sick, I will. I'll be 'cross de plain to de edge of de forest by time dark comes. Once in de woods in de night, dey got a swell chance o' findin' dis baby! Dawn tomorrow I'll be out at de oder side and on de coast whar dat French gunboat is stayin'. She picks me up, take me to Martinique when she go dar, and dere I is safe wid a mighty big bankroll in my jeans. It's easy as rollin' off a log.

SMITHERS [*Maliciously*]: But s'posin' somethin' 'appens wrong an' they do nab yer?

JONES [*Decisively*]: Dey don't—dat's de answer.

SMITHERS: But, just for argyment's sake—what'd you do?

JONES [*Frowning*]: I'se got five lead bullets in dis gun good enuff fo' common bush niggers—and after dat I got de silver bullet left to cheat 'em out o' gittin' me.

SMITHERS [*Jeeringly*]: Ho, I was fergettin' that silver bullet. You'll bump yourself orf in style, won't yer? Blimey!

JONES [*Gloomily*]: You kin bet yo whole roll on one thing, white man. Dis baby plays out his string to de end and when he quits, he quits wid a bang de way he ought. Silver bullet ain't none too good for him when he go, dat's a fac'! [*Then shaking off his nervousness—with a confident laugh*] Sho'! What is I talkin' about? Ain't come to dat yit and I never will—not wid trash niggers like dese yere. [*Boastfully*] Silver bullet bring me luck anyway. I kin outguess, outrun, outfight, an' outplay de whole lot o' dem all ovah de board any time o' de day er night! You watch me! [*From the distant hills comes the faint, steady thump of a tom-tom, low and vibrating. It starts at a rate exactly corresponding to normal pulse beat—72 to the minute—and contin-*

ues at a gradually accelerating rate from this point
uninterruptedly to the very end of the play.]

[JONES *starts at the sound. A strange look of appre-*
hension creeps into his face for a moment as he lis-
tens. Then he asks, with an attempt to regain his
most casual manner]:   What's dat drum beatin'
fo'?

SMITHERS [*With a mean grin*]:   For you. That means
the bleedin' ceremony 'as started. I've 'eard it before
and I knows.

JONES: Cer'mony? What cer'mony?

SMITHERS: The blacks is 'oldin' a bloody meetin',
'avin' a war dance, gettin' their courage worked up
b'fore they starts after you.

JONES: Let dem! Dey'll sho' need it!

SMITHERS: And they're there 'oldin' their 'eather
religious service—makin' no end of devil spells and
charms to 'elp 'em against your silver bullet. [*He*
guffaws loudly.] Blimey, but they're balmy as 'ell!

JONES [*A tiny bit awed and shaken in spite of*
himself]:   Huh! Takes more'n dat to scare dis
chicken!

SMITHERS [*Scenting the other's feeling—maliciously*]:
Ternight when it's pitch black in the forest, they'll
'ave their pet devils and ghosts 'oundin' after you.
You'll find yer bloody 'air 'll be standin' on end
before termorrow mornin'. [*Seriously*] It's a bleedin'
queer place, that stinkin' forest, even in daylight.
Yer don't know what might 'appen in there, it's that
rotten still. Always sends the cold shivers down my
back minute I gets in it.

JONES [*With a contemptuous sniff*]:   I ain't no
chicken-liver like you is. Trees an' me, we'se friends
and dar's a full moon comin' bring me light. And
let dem po' niggers make all de fool spells dey'se a
min' to. Does yo' s'pect I'se silly enuff to b'lieve in
ghosts an' ha'ants an' all dat ole woman's talk?

G'long, white man! You ain't talkin' to me. [*With a chuckle*] Doesn't you know dey's got to do wid a man was member in good standin' o' de Baptist Church? Sho' I was dat when I was porter on de Pullmans, befo' I gits into my little trouble. Let dem try deir heathen tricks. De Baptist Church done pertect me and land dem all in hell. [*Then with more confident satisfaction*] And I'se got little silver bullet o' my own, don't forgit.

SMITHERS: Ho! You 'aven't give much 'eed to your Baptist Church since you been down 'ere. I've 'eard myself you 'ad turned yer coat an' was takin' up with their blarsted witch-doctors, or whatever the 'ell yer calls the swine.

JONES [*Vehemently*]: I pretends to! Sho' I pretends! Dat's part o' my game from de fust. If I finds out dem niggers believes dat black is white, den I yells it out louder 'n deir loudest. It don't git me nothin' to do missionary work for de Baptist Church. I'se after de coin, an' I lays my Jesus on de shelf for de time bein'. [*Stops abruptly to look at his watch—alertly*] But I ain't got de time to waste no more fool talk wid you. I'se gwine away from heah dis secon'. [*He reaches in under the throne and pulls out an expensive Panama hat with a bright multi-colored band and sets it jauntily on his head.*] So long, white man! [*With a grin*] See you in jail sometime, maybe!

SMITHERS: Not me, you won't. Well, I wouldn't be in your bloody boots for no bloomin' money, but 'ere's wishin' yer luck just the same.

JONES [*Contemptuously*]: You're de frightenedest man evah I see! I tells you I'se safe's 'f I was in New York City. It takes dem niggers from now to dark to git up de nerve to start somethin'. By dat time, I'se got a head start dey never kotch up wid.

SMITHERS [*Maliciously*]: Give my regards to any ghosts yer meets up with.

JONES [*Grinning*]: If dat ghost got money, I'll tell him never ha'nt you less'n he wants to lose it.

SMITHERS [*Flattered*]: Garn! [*Then curiously*] Ain't yer takin' no luggage with yer?

JONES: I travels light when I want to move fast. And I got tinned grub buried on de edge o' de forest. [*Boastfully*] Now say that I don't look ahead an' use my brains! [*With a wide, liberal gesture*] I will all dat's left in de palace to you—and you better grab all you kin sneak away wid befo' dey gits here.

SMITHERS [*Gratefully*]: Righto—and thanks ter yer. [*As* JONES *walks toward the door in rear—cautioningly*] Say! Look 'ere, you ain't goin' out that way, are yer?

JONES: Does you think I'd slink out de back door like a common nigger? I'se Emperor yit, ain't I? And de Emperor Jones leaves de way he comes, and dat black trash don't dare stop him—not yit, leastways. [*He stops for a moment in the doorway, listening to the far-off but insistent beat of the tom-tom*] Listen to dat roll-call, will you? Must be mighty big drum carry dat far. [*Then with a laugh*] Well, if dey ain't no whole brass band to see me off, I sho' got de drum part of it. So long, white man. [*He puts his hands in his pockets and with studied carelessness, whistling a tune, he saunters out of the doorway and off to the left.*]

SMITHERS [*Looks after him with a puzzled admiration*]: 'E's got 'ise bloomin' nerve with 'im, s'elp me! [*Then angrily*] Ho—the bleedin' nigger—puttin' on 'is bloody airs! I 'opes they nabs 'im an' gives 'im what's what! [*Then putting business before the pleasure of this thought, looking around him with cupidity*] A bloke ought to find a 'ole lot in this palace that'd go for a bit of cash. Let's take a look, 'Arry, me lad. [*He starts for the doorway on right as*

The curtain falls.]

Scene Two

Nightfall. The end of the plain where the Great Forest begins. The foreground is sandy, level ground dotted by a few stones and clumps of stunted bushes cowering close against the earth to escape the buffeting of the trade wind. In the rear the forest is a wall of darkness dividing the world. Only when the eye becomes accustomed to the gloom can the outlines of separate trunks of the nearest trees be made out, enormous pillars of deeper blackness. A somber monotone of wind lost in the leaves moans in the air. Yet this sound serves but to intensify the impression of the forest's relentless immobility, to form a background throwing into relief its brooding, implacable silence.

[JONES *enters from the left, walking rapidly. He stops as he nears the edge of the forest, looks around him quickly, peering into the dark as if searching for some familiar landmark. Then, apparently satisfied that he is where he ought to be, he throws himself on the ground, dog-tired.*]

JONES: Well, heah I is. In de nick o' time, too! Little mo' an' it'd be blacker'n de ace of spades heah-abouts. [*He pulls a bandana handkerchief from his hip pocket and mops off his perspiring face.*] Sho'! Gimme air! I'se tuckered out sho' nuff. Dat soft Emperor job ain't no trainin' fo' a long hike ovah dat plain in de brilin' sun. [*Then with a chuckle*] Cheah up, nigger, de worst is yet to come. [*He lifts his head and stares at the forest. His chuckle peters out abruptly. In a tone of awe*] My goodness, look at dem woods, will you? Dat no-count Smithers said dey'd be black an' he sho' called de turn. [*Turning away from them quickly and looking down at his feet, he snatches at a chance to change the subject— solicitously.*] Feet, you is holdin' up yo' end fine an' I sutinly hopes you ain't blisterin' none. It's time you git a rest. [*He takes off his shoes, his eyes studiously avoiding the forest. He feels of the soles of his feet gingerly.*] You is still in de pink—on'y a little mite feverish. Cool yo'selfs. Remember you done got a long journey yit befo' you. [*He sits in a weary attitude, listening to the rhythmic beating of the tom-tom. He grumbles in a loud tone to cover up a growing uneasiness.*] Bush niggers! Wonder dey wouldn' git sick o' beatin' dat drum. Sound louder, seem like. I wonder if dey's startin' after me? [*He scrambles to his feet, looking back across the plain.*] Couldn't see dem now, nohow, if dey was hundred feet away. [*Then shaking himself like a wet dog to get rid of these depressing thoughts*] Sho', dey's miles an' miles behind. What you gittin' fidgety about? [*But he sits down and begins to lace up his shoes in great haste, all the time muttering reassuringly.*] You know what? Yo' belly is empty, dat's what's de matter wid you. Come time to eat! Wid nothin' but wind on yo' stumach, o' course you feels jiggedy. Well, we eats right heah an' now soon's I gits dese pesky shoes laced up! [*He finishes lacing up his shoes.*] Dere! Now le's see. [*Gets on his hands and knees and searches the ground around him with his eyes*] White stone, white stone, where is you? [*He sees the first white stone and crawls to it—with satisfaction.*] Heah you is! I

knowed dis was de right place. Box of grub, come
to me. [*He turns over the stone and feels under it—
in a tone of dismay.*] Ain't heah! Gorry, is I in de
right place or isn't I? Dere's 'nother stone. Guess
dat's it. [*He scrambles to the next stone and turns
it over.*] Ain't heah, neither! Grub, whar is you?
Ain't heah. Gorry, has I got to go hungry into dem
woods—all de night? [*While he is talking he scrambles from one stone to another, turning them over
in frantic haste. Finally, he jumps to his feet excitedly.*] Is I lost de place? Must have! But how dat
happen when I was followin' de trail across de plain
in broad daylight? [*Almost plaintively*] I'se hungry,
I is! I gotta git my feed. Whar's my strength gonna
come from if I doesn't? Gorry, I gotta find dat grub
high an' low somehow! Why it come dark so quick
like dat? Can't see nothin'. [*He scratches a match
on his trousers and peers about him. The rate of the
beat of the far-off tom-tom increases perceptibly as
he does so. He mutters in a bewildered voice.*] How
come all dese white stones come heah when I only
remembers one? [*Suddenly, with a frightened grasp,
he flings the match on the ground and stamps on
it.*] Nigger, is you gone crazy mad? Is you lightin'
matches to show dem whar you is? Fo' Lawd's sake,
use yo' haid. Gorry, I'se got to be careful! [*He stares
at the plain behind him apprehensively, his hand on
his revolver.*] But how come all dese white stones?
And whar's dat tin box o' grub I had all wrapped
up in oil cloth?

[*While his back is turned, the* LITTLE FORMLESS FEARS
*creep out from the deeper blackness of the forest. They
are black, shapeless, only their glittering little eyes can
be seen. If they have any describable form at all it is
that of a grubworm about the size of a creeping child.
They move noiselessly, but with deliberate, painful ef-*

fort, striving to raise themselves on end, failing and sinking prone again. JONES *turns about to face the forest. He stares up at the tops of the trees, seeking vainly to discover his whereabouts by their conformation.*]

Can't tell nothin' from dem trees! Gorry, nothin' 'round heah look like I evah seed it befo'. I'se done lost de place sho' 'nuff! [*With mournful foreboding*] It's mighty queer! It's mighty queer! [*With sudden forced defiance—in an angry tone*] Woods, is you tryin' to put somethin' ovah on me?
[*From the formless creatures on the ground in front of him comes a tiny gale of low mocking laughter like a rustling of leaves. They squirm upward toward him in twisted attitudes.* JONES *looks down, leaps backward with a yell of terror, yanking out his revolver as he does so—in a quavering voice*] What's dat? Who's dar? What is you? Git away from me befo' I shoots you up! You don't? . . .

[*He fires. There is a flash, a loud report, then silence broken only by the far-off, quickened throb of the tom-tom. The formless creatures have scurried back into the forest.* JONES *remains fixed in his position, listening intently. The sound of the shot, the reassuring feel of the revolver in his hand, have somewhat restored his shaken nerve. He addresses himself with renewed confidence.*]

Dey're gone. Dat shot fix 'em. Dey was only little animals—little wild pigs, I reckon. Dey've maybe rooted out yo' grub an' eat it. Sho', you fool nigger, what you think dey is—ha'nts? [*Excitedly*] Gorry, you give de game away when you fire dat shot. Dem niggers heah dat fo' su'tin! Time you beat in de woods widout no long waits. [*He starts for the forest—hesitates before the plunge—then urging himself in with manful resolution.*] Git in, nigger! What you skeered at? Ain't nothin' dere but de trees! Git in! [*He plunges boldly into the forest.*]

Scene Three

*Nine o'clock. In the forest. The moon has just risen.
It beams, drifting through the canopy of leaves, makes
a barely perceptible, suffused, eerie glow. A dense low
wall of underbrush and creepers is in the nearer fore-
ground, fencing in a small triangular clearing. Beyond
this is the massed blackness of the forest like an en-
compassing barrier. A path is dimly discerned leading
down to the clearing from left, rear, and winding away
from it again toward the right. As the scene opens
nothing can be distinctly made out. Except for the
beating of the tom-tom, which is a trifle louder and
quicker than in the previous scene, there is silence,
broken every few seconds by a queer, clicking sound.
Then gradually the figure of the Negro,* JEFF, *can be
discerned crouching on his haunches at the rear of the
triangle. He is middle-aged, thin, brown in color, is
dressed in a Pullman porter's uniform, cap, etc. He is
throwing a pair of dice on the ground before him,
picking them up, shaking them, casting them out with
the regular, rigid, mechanical movements of an autom-
aton. The heavy, plodding footsteps of someone approaching along the trail from the left are heard and*
JONES' *voice, pitched in a slightly higher key and
strained in a cheering effort to overcome its own trem-
ors.*

JONES: De moon's rizen. Does you heah dat, nigger?
You gits more light from dis out. No mo' buttin'

yo' fool head agin' de trunks an' scratchin' de hide
off yo' legs in de bushes. Now you sees whar yo'se
gwine. So cheer up! From now on you has a snap.
[*He steps just to the rear of the triangular clearing
and mops off his face on his sleeve. He has lost his
Panama hat. His face is scratched, his brilliant uniform shows several large rents.*] What time's it gittin' to be, I wonder? I dassent light no match to find
out. Phoo'. It's wa'm an' dat's a fac'! [*Wearily*] How
long I been makin' tracks in dese woods? Must be
hours an' hours. Seems like fo'evah! Yit can't be,
when de moon's jes' riz. Dis am a long night fo' yo',
yo' Majesty! [*With a mournful chuckle*] Majesty!
Der ain't much majesty 'bout dis baby now. [*With
attempted cheerfulness*] Never min'. It's all part o'
de game. Dis night come to an end like everything
else. And when you gits dar safe and has dat bankroll in yo' hands you laughs at all dis. [*He starts to
whistle but checks himself abruptly.*] What yo'
whistlin' for, you po' dope! Want all de worl' to
heah you? [*He stops talking to listen.*] Heah dat ole
drum! Sho' gits nearer from de sound. Dey're
packin' it along wid 'em. Time fo' me to move. [*He
takes a step forward, then stops—worriedly.*]
What's dat odder queer clickety sound I heah? Dere
it is! Sound close! Sound like—sound like—Fo' God
sake, sound like some nigger was shootin' crap!
[*Frightenedly*] I better beat it quick when I gits dem
notions. [*He walks quickly into the clear space—
then stands transfixed as he sees* JEFF—*in a terrified
gasp*] Who dar? Who dat? It dat you, Jeff? [*Starting
toward the other, forgetful for a moment of his sur-
roundings and really believing it is a living man that
he sees—in a tone of happy relief*] Jeff! I'se sho'
mighty glad to see you! Dey tol' me you done died
from dat razor cut I gives you. [*Stopping suddenly,
bewilderedly*] But how you come to be heah, nigger?

[*He stares fascinatedly at the other who continues his mechanical play with the dice.* JONES' *eyes begin to roll wildly. He stutters.*] Ain't you gwine—look up—can't you speaks to me? Is you—is you—a ha'nt? [*He jerks out his revolver in a frenzy of terrified rage.*] Nigger, I kills you dead once. Has I got to kill you again? You take it den. [*He fires. When the smoke clears away* JEFF *has disappeared.* JONES *stands trembling—then with a certain reassurance*] He's gone, anyway. Ha'nt or no ha'nt, dat shot fix him. [*The beat of the far-off tom-tom is perceptibly louder and more rapid.* JONES *becomes conscious of it—with a start, looking back over his shoulder.*] Dey's gittin' near! Dey's comin' fast! And heah I is shootin' shots to let 'em know jes' whar I is. Oh, Gorry, I'se got to run. [*Forgetting the path he plunges wildly into the underbrush in the rear and disappears in the shadow.*]

Scene Four

Eleven o'clock. In the forest. A wide dirt road runs diagonally from right, front, to left, rear. Rising sheer on both sides the forest walls it in. The moon is now up. Under its light the road glimmers ghastly and unreal. It is as if the forest had stood aside momentarily to let the road pass through and accomplish its veiled purpose. This done, the forest will fold in upon itself again and the road will be no more. JONES *stumbles in from the forest on the right. His uniform is ragged and torn. He looks about him with numbed surprise when he sees the road, his eyes blinking in the bright moonlight. He flops down exhaustedly and pants heavily for a while. Then with sudden anger*

JONES: I'm meltin' wid heat! Runnin' an' runnin' an' runnin'! Damn dis heah coat! Like a strait-jacket! [*He tears off his coat and flings it away from him, revealing himself stripped to the waist.*] Dere! Dat's better! Now I kin breathe! [*Looking down at his feet, the spurs catch his eye.*] And to hell wid dese high-fangled spurs. Dey're what's been a-trippin' me up an' breakin' my neck. [*He unstraps them and flings them away disgustedly.*] Dere! I gits rid o' dem frippety Emperor trappin's an' I travels lighter. Lawd! I'se tired! [*After a pause, listening to the insistent beat of the tom-tom in the distance*] I must 'a put some distance between myself an' dem—runnin' like dat—and yit—dat damn drum sounds jes'

138

de same—nearer, even. Well, I guess I a'most holds
my lead anyhow. Dey won't never catch up. [*With
a sigh*] If on'y my fool legs stands up. Oh, I'se sorry
I evah went in for dis. Dat Emperor's job is sho'
hard to shake. [*He looks around him suspiciously.*]
How'd this road evah git heah? Good level road,
too. I never remembers seein' it befo'. [*Shaking his
head apprehensively*] Dese woods is sho' full o' de
queerest things at night. [*With a sudden terror*]
Lawd God, don't let me see no more o' dem ha'nts!
Dey gits my goat! [*Then trying to talk himself into
confidence*] Ha'nts! You fool nigger, dey ain't no
such things! Don't de Baptist parson tell you dat
many times? Is you civilized, or is you like dese
ign'rent black niggers heah? Sho'! Dat was all in yo'
own head. Wasn't nothin' dere. Wasn't no Jeff!
Know what? You jus' get seein' dem things 'cause
yo' belly's empty and you's sick wid hunger inside.
Hunger 'fects yo' head and yo' eyes. Any fool know
dat. [*Then pleading fervently*] But bless God, I don't
come across no more o' dem, whatever dey is! [*Then
cautiously*] Rest! Don't talk! Rest! You needs it.
Den you gits on yo' way again. [*Looking at the
moon*] Night's half gone a'most. You hits de coast
in de mawning! Den you'se all safe.

[*From the right forward a small gang of* NEGROES *en-
ter. They are dressed in striped convict suits, their
heads are shaven, one leg drags limpingly, shackled to
a heavy ball and chain. Some carry picks, the others
shovels. They are followed by a white man dressed in
the uniform of a prison guard. A Winchester rifle is
slung across his shoulders and he carries a heavy whip.
At a signal from the* GUARD *they stop on the road
opposite where* JONES *is sitting.* JONES, *who has been
staring up at the sky, unmindful of their noiseless approach, suddenly looks down and sees them. His eyes*

pop out, he tries to get to his feet and fly, but sinks back, too numbed by fright to move. His voice catches in a choking prayer]

Lawd Jesus!

[*The* PRISON GUARD *cracks his whip—noiselessly— and at that signal all the convicts start to work on the road. They swing their picks, they shovel, but not a sound comes from their labor. Their movements, like those of* JEFF *in the preceding scene, are those of automatons—rigid, slow, and mechanical. The* PRISON GUARD *points sternly at* JONES *with his whip, motions him to take his place among the other shovelers.* JONES *gets to his feet in a hypnotized stupor. He mumbles subserviently.*]

Yes, suh! Yes, suh! I'se comin'.

[*As he shuffles, dragging one foot, over to his place, he curses under his breath with rage and hatred.*]

God damn yo' soul, I gits even wid you yit, sometime.

[*As if there were a shovel in his hands he goes through weary, mechanical gestures of digging up dirt, and throwing it to the roadside. Suddenly the* GUARD *approaches him angrily, threateningly. He raises his whip and lashes* JONES *viciously across the shoulders with it.* JONES *winces with pain and cowers abjectly. The* GUARD *turns his back on him and walks away contemptuously. Instantly* JONES *straightens up. With arms upraised as if his shovel were a club in his hands he springs murderously at the unsuspecting* GUARD. *In the act of crashing down his shovel on the white man's skull,* JONES *suddenly becomes aware that his hands are empty. He cries despairingly.*]

Whar's my shovel? Gimme my shovel till I splits his damn head! [*Appealing to his fellow convicts*] Gimme a shovel, one o' you, fo' God's sake!

[*They stand fixed in motionless attitudes, their eyes on the ground. The* GUARD *seems to wait expectantly, his back turned to the attacker.* JONES *bellows with baffled, terrified rage, tugging frantically at his revolver.*]

I kills you, you white debil, if it's de last thing I evah does! Ghost or debil, I kill you again!

[*He frees the revolver and fires point blank at the* GUARD'S *back. Instantly the walls of the forest close in from both sides, the road and the figures of the convict gang are blotted out in an enshrouding darkness. The only sounds are a crashing in the underbrush as* JONES *leaps away in mad flight and the throbbing of the tom-tom, still far distant, but increased in volume of sound and rapidity of beat.*]

Scene Five

One o'clock. A large circular clearing, enclosed by the serried ranks of gigantic trunks of tall trees whose tops are lost to view. In the center is a big dead stump worn by time into a curious resemblance to an auction block. The moon floods the clearing with a clear light. JONES *forces his way in through the forest on the left. He looks wildly about the clearing with hunted, fearful glances. His pants are in tatters, his shoes cut and misshapen, flapping about his feet. He slinks cautiously to the stump in the center and sits down in a tense position, ready for instant flight. Then he holds his head in his hands and rocks back and forth, moaning to himself miserably.*

JONES: Oh Lawd, Lawd! Oh Lawd, Lawd! [*Suddenly he throws himself on his knees and raises his clasped hands to the sky—in a voice of agonized pleading.*] Lawd Jesus, heah my prayer! I'se a po' sinner, a po' sinner! I knows I done wrong, I knows it! When I cotches Jeff cheatin' wid loaded dice my anger overcomes me and I kills him dead! Lawd, I done wrong! When dat guard hits me wid de whip, my anger overcomes me, and I kills him dead. Lawd, I done wrong! And down heah whar dese fool bush niggers raises me up to the seat o' de mighty, I steals all I could grab. Lawd, I done wrong! I knows it! I'se sorry! Forgive me, Lawd! Forgive dis po' sinner! [*Then beseeching terrifiedly*] And keep dem away,

Lawd! Keep dem away from me! And stop dat drum soundin' in my ears! Dat begin to sound ha'nted, too. [*He gets to his feet, evidently slightly reassured by his prayer—with attempted confidence*] De Lawd'll preserve me from dem ha'nts after dis. [*Sits down on the stump again*] I ain't skeered o' real men. Let dem come. But dem odders . . . [*He shudders—then looks down at his feet, working his toes inside the shoes—with a groan.*] Oh, my po' feet! Dem shoes ain't no use no more 'ceptin' to hurt. I'se better off widout dem. [*He unlaces them and pulls them off—holds the wrecks of the shoes in his hands and regards them mournfully*] You was real, A-one patin' leather, too. Look at you now. Emperor, you'se gittin' mighty low!

[*He sits dejectedly and remains with bowed shoulders, staring down at the shoes in his hands as if reluctant to throw them away. While his attention is thus occupied, a crowd of figures silently enters the clearing from all sides. All are dressed in Southern costumes of the period of the fifties of the last century. There are middle-aged men who are evidently well-to-do planters. There is one spruce, authoritative individual—the* AUCTIONEER. *There is a crowd of curious spectators, chiefly young belles and dandies who have come to the slave-market for diversion. All exchange courtly greetings in dumb show and chat silently together. There is something stiff, rigid, unreal, marionettish about their movements. They group themselves about the stump. Finally a batch of slaves are led in from the left by an attendant—three men of different ages, two women, one with a baby in her arms, nursing. They are placed to the left of the stump, beside* JONES. *The white planters look them over appraisingly as if they were cattle, and exchange judgments on each. The dandies point with their fingers and make witty* remarks. *The belles titter bewitchingly. All this in silence save for the ominous throb of the tom-tom. The* AUCTIONEER *holds up his hand, taking his place at the stump. The group strain forward attentively. He touches* JONES *on the shoulder peremptorily, motioning for him to stand on the stump—the auction block.*

JONES *looks up, sees the figures on all sides, looks wildly for some opening to escape, sees none, screams and leaps madly to the top of the stump to get as far away from them as possible. He stands there, cowering, paralyzed with horror. The* AUCTIONEER *begins his silent spiel. He points to* JONES, *appeals to the planters to see for themselves. Here is a good field hand, sound in wind and limb as they can see. Very strong still in spite of his being middle-aged. Look at that back. Look at those shoulders. Look at the muscles in his arms and his sturdy legs. Capable of any amount of hard labor. Moreover, of a good disposition, intelligent and tractable. Will any gentleman start the bidding? The* PLANTERS *raise their fingers, make their bids. They are apparently all eager to possess* JONES. *The bidding is lively, the crowd interested. While this has been going on,* JONES *has been seized by the courage of desperation. He dares to look down and around him. Over his face abject terror gives way to mystification, to gradual realization—stutteringly]*

What you all doin', white folks? What's all dis? What you all lookin' at me fo'? What you doin' wid me, anyhow? [*Suddenly convulsed with raging hatred and fear*] Is dis a auction? Is you sellin' me like dey uster befo' de war? [*Jerking out his revolver just as the* AUCTIONEER *knocks him down to one of the planters—glaring from him to the purchaser*] And *you* sells me? And *you* buys me? I shows you I'se a free nigger, damn yo' souls! [*He fires at the* AUCTIONEER *and at the*

PLANTER *with such rapidity that the two shots are almost simultaneous. As if this were a signal the walls of the forest fold in. Only blackness remains and silence broken by* JONES *as he rushes off, crying with fear—and by the quickened, ever louder beat of the tom-tom.*]

Scene Six

*Three o'clock. A cleared space in the forest. The limbs
of the trees meet over it forming a low ceiling about
five feet from the ground. The interlocked ropes of
creepers reaching upward to entwine the tree trunks
give an arched appearance to the sides. The space thus
enclosed is like the dark, noisome hold of some an-
cient vessel. The moonlight is almost completely shut
out and only a vague, wan light filters through. There
is the noise of someone approaching from the left,
stumbling and crawling through the undergrowth.*
JONES' *voice is heard between chattering moans.*

JONES: Oh, Lawd, what I gwine do now? Ain't got
   no bullet left on'y de silver one. If mo' o' dem ha'nts
   come after me, how I gwine skeer dem away? Oh,
   Lawd, on'y de silver one left—an' I gotta save dat
   fo' luck. If I shoots dat one I'm a goner sho'! Lawd,
   it's black heah! Whar's de moon? Oh, Lawd, don't
   dis night evah come to an end? [*By the sounds, he
   is feeling his way cautiously forward.*] Dere! Dis
   feels like a clear space. I gotta lie down an' rest. I
   don't care if dem niggers does cotch me. I gotta rest.

[*He is well forward now where his figure can be dimly
made out. His pants have been so torn away that what
is left of them is no better than a breech cloth. He
flings himself full length, face downward on the
ground, panting with exhaustion. Gradually it seems
to grow lighter in the enclosed space and two rows of*

146

seated figures can be seen behind JONES. *They are sitting in crumbled, despairing attitudes, hunched, facing one another with their backs touching the forest walls as if they were shackled to them. All are Negroes, naked save for loin cloths. At first they are silent and motionless. Then they begin to sway slowly forward toward each other and back again in unison, as if they were laxly letting themselves follow the long roll of a ship at sea. At the same time, a low, melancholy murmur rises among them, increasing gradually by rhythmic degrees which seem to be directed and controlled by the throb of the tom-tom in the distance, to a long, tremulous wail of despair that reaches a certain pitch, unbearably acute, then falls by slow gradations of tone into silence and is taken up again.* JONES *starts, looks up, sees the figures, and throws himself down again to shut out the sight. A shudder of terror shakes his whole body as the wail rises up about him again. But the next time, his voice, as if under some uncanny compulsion, starts with the others. As their chorus lifts he rises to a sitting posture similar to the others, swaying back and forth. His voice reaches the highest pitch of sorrow, of desolation. The light fades out, the other voices cease, and only darkness is left.* JONES *can be heard scrambling to his feet and running off, his voice sinking down the scale and receding as he moves farther and farther away in the forest. The tom-tom beats louder, quicker, with a more insistent, triumphant pulsation.*]

Scene Seven

*Five o'clock. The foot of a gigantic tree by the edge
of a great river. A rough structure of boulders, like an
altar, is by the tree. The raised river bank is in the
nearer background. Beyond this the surface of the
river spreads out, brilliant and unruffled in the moonlight, blotted out and merged into a veil of bluish mist
in the distance.* JONES' *voice is heard from the left rising and falling in the long, despairing wail of the
chained slaves, to the rhythmic beat of the tom-tom.
As his voice sinks into silence, he enters the open
space. The expression of his face is fixed and stony,
his eyes have an obsessed glare, he moves with a
strange deliberation like a sleepwalker or one in a
trance. He looks around at the tree, the rough stone
altar, the moonlit surface of the river beyond, and
passes his hand over his head with a vague gesture of
puzzled bewilderment. Then, as if in obedience to
some obscure impulse, he sinks into a kneeling, de-
votional posture before the altar. Then he seems to
come to himself partly, to have an uncertain realization of what he is doing, for he straightens up and
stares about him horrifiedly—in an incoherent mum-
ble*

JONES: What—what is I doin'? What is—dis place?
Seems like—seems like I know dat tree—an' dem
stones—an' de river. I remember—seems like I ben

148

heah befo'. [*Tremblingly*] Oh, Gorry, I'se skeered in dis place! I'se skeered! Oh, Lawd, pertect dis sinner!

[*Crawling away from the altar, he cowers close to the ground, his face hidden, his shoulders heaving with sobs of hysterical fright. From behind the trunk of the tree, as if he had sprung out of it, the figure of the* CONGO WITCH-DOCTOR *appears. He is wizened and old, naked except for the fur of some small animal tied about his waist, its bushy tail hanging down in front. His body is stained all over a bright red. Antelope horns are on each side of his head, branching upward. In one hand he carries a bone rattle, in the other a charm stick with a bunch of white cockatoo feathers tied to the end. A great number of glass beads and bone ornaments are about his neck, ears, wrists, and ankles. He struts noiselessly with a queer prancing step to a position in the clear ground between* JONES *and the altar. Then with a preliminary, summoning stamp of his foot on the earth, he begins to dance and to chant. As if in response to his summons the beating of the tom-tom grows to a fierce, exultant boom whose throbs seem to fill the air with vibrating rhythm.* JONES *looks up, starts to spring to his feet, reaches a half-kneeling, half-squatting position and remains rigidly fixed there, paralyzed with awed fascination by this new apparition. The* WITCH-DOCTOR *sways, stamping with his foot, his bone rattle clicking the time. His voice rises and falls in a weird, monotonous croon, without articulate word divisions. Gradually his dance becomes clearly one of a narrative in pantomime, his croon is an incantation, a charm to allay the fierceness of some implacable deity demanding sacrifice. He flees, he is pursued by devils, he hides, he flees again. Ever wilder and wilder becomes his flight, nearer and nearer draws the pursuing evil, more and more the spirit of terror gains possession of him. His croon, rising to intensity, is punctuated by shrill cries.* JONES *has become completely hypnotized. His voice joins in the incantation, in the cries, he beats time with his hands and sways his body to and fro from the waist. The whole spirit and meaning of the dance has entered into him, has become his spirit. Finally the theme of the pantomime halts on a howl of despair, and is taken up again in a note of savage hope. There is a salvation. The forces of evil demand sacrifice. They must be appeased. The* WITCH-DOCTOR *points with his wand to the sacred tree, to the river beyond, to the altar, and finally to* JONES *with a ferocious command.* JONES *seems to sense the meaning of this. It is he who must offer himself for sacrifice. He beats his forehead abjectly to the ground, moaning hysterically.*]

Mercy, Oh Lawd! Mercy! Mercy on dis po' sinner.

[*The* WITCH-DOCTOR *springs to the river bank. He stretches out his arms and calls to some god within its depths. Then he starts backward slowly, his arms remaining out. A huge head of a crocodile appears over the bank and its eyes, glittering greenly, fasten upon* JONES. *He stares into them fascinatedly. The* WITCH-DOCTOR *prances up to him, touches him with his wand, motions with hideous command toward the waiting monster.* JONES *squirms on his belly nearer and nearer, moaning continually.*]

Mercy, Lawd! Mercy!

[*The crocodile heaves more of his enormous hulk onto the land.* JONES *squirms toward him. The* WITCH-DOCTOR'S *voice shrills out in furious exultation, the tom-tom beats madly.* JONES *cries out in a fierce, exhausted spasm of anguished pleading.*]

Lawd, save me! Lawd Jesus, heah my prayer!

[*Immediately, in answer to his prayer, comes the thought of the one bullet left him. He snatches at his hip, shouting defiantly.*]

De silver bullet! You don't git me yit!

[*He fires at the green eyes in front of him. The head of the crocodile sinks back behind the river bank, the* WITCH-DOCTOR *springs behind the sacred tree and disappears.* JONES *lies with his face to the ground, his arms outstretched, whimpering with fear as the throb of the tom-tom fills the silence about him with a somber pulsation, a baffled but revengeful power.*]

Scene Eight

Dawn. Same as Scene Two, the dividing line of forest and plain. The nearest tree trunks are dimly revealed but the forest behind them is still a mass of glooming shadows. The tom-tom seems on the very spot, so loud and continuously vibrating are its beats. LEM *enters from the left, followed by a small squad of his soldiers, and by the Cockney trader,* SMITHERS. LEM *is a heavy-set, ape-faced old savage of the extreme African type, dressed only in a loin cloth. A revolver and cartridge belt are about his waist. His soldiers are in different degrees of rag-concealed nakedness. All wear broad palm-leaf hats. Each one carries a rifle.* SMITHERS *is the same as in Scene One. One of the soldiers, evidently a tracker, is peering about keenly on the ground. He grunts and points at the spot where* JONES *entered the forest.* LEM *and* SMITHERS *come to look.*

SMITHERS [*After a glance, turns away in disgust*]: That's where 'e went in right enough. Much good it'll do yer. 'E's miles orf by this an' safe to the Coast, damn 'is 'ide! I tole yer yer'd lose 'im, didn't I?—wastin' the 'ole bloomin' night beatin' yer bloody drum and castin' yer silly spells! Gawd blimey, wot a pack!

LEM [*Gutturally*]: We cotch him. You see. [*He makes a motion to his soldiers who squat down on their haunches in a semicircle.*]

SMITHERS [*Exasperatedly*]: Well, ain't yer goin' in

152

an' 'unt 'im in the woods? What the 'ell's the good of waitin'?

LEM [*Imperturbably—squatting down himself*]: We cotch him.

SMITHERS [*Turning away from him contemptuously*]: Aw! Garn! 'E's a better man than the lot o' you put together. I 'ates the sight of 'im but I'll say that for 'im. [*A sound of snapping twigs comes from the forest. The soldiers jump to their feet, cocking their rifles alertly.* LEM *remains sitting with an imperturbable expression, but listening intently. The sound from the woods is repeated.* LEM *makes a quick signal with his hand. His followers creep quickly but noiselessly into the forest, scattering so that each enters at a different spot.*]

SMITHERS [*In the silence that follows—in a contemptuous whisper*]: You ain't thinkin' that would be 'im, I 'ope?

LEM [*Calmly*]: We cotch him.

SMITHERS: Blarsted fat 'eads! [*Then after a second's thought—wonderingly*] Still an' all, it might 'appen. If 'e lost 'is bloody way in these stinkin' woods 'e'd likely turn in a circle without 'is knowin' it. They all does.

LEM [*Peremptorily*]: Sssh! [*The reports of several rifles sound from the forest, followed a second later by savage, exultant yells. The beating of the tom-tom abruptly ceases.* LEM *looks up at the white man with a grin of satisfaction.*] We cotch him. Him dead.

SMITHERS [*With a snarl*]: 'Ow d'yer know it's 'im an' 'ow d'yer know 'e's dead?

LEM: My mens dey got 'um silver bullets. Dey kill him shore.

SMITHERS [*Astonished*]: They got silver bullets?

LEM: Lead bullet no kill him. He got 'um strong

charm. I cook 'um money, make 'um silver bullet, make 'um strong charm, too.

SMITHERS [*Light breaking upon him*]: So that's wot you was up to all night, wot? You was scared to put after 'im till you'd moulded silver bullets, eh?

LEM [*Simply stating a fact*]: Yes. Him got strong charm. Lead no good.

SMITHERS [*Slapping his thigh and guffawing*]: Haw-haw! If yer don't beat all 'ell! [*Then recovering himself—scornfully*] I'll bet yer it ain't 'im they shot at all, yer bleedin' looney!

LEM [*Calmly*]: Dey come bring him now. [*The soldiers come out of the forest, carrying* JONES' *limp body. There is a little reddish-purple hole under his left breast. He is dead. They carry him to* LEM, *who examines his body with great satisfaction.* SMITHERS *leans over his shoulder—in a tone of frightened awe.*] Well, they did for yer right enough, Jonsey, me lad! Dead as a 'erring! [*Mockingly*] Where's yer 'igh an' mighty airs now, yer bloomin' Majesty? [*Then with a grin*] Silver bullets! Gawd blimey, but yer died in the 'eight o' style, any'ow! [LEM *makes a motion to the soldiers to carry the body out left.* SMITHERS *speaks to him sneeringly.*]

SMITHERS: And I s'pose you think it's yer bleedin' charms and yer silly beatin' the drum that made 'im run in a circle when 'e'd lost 'imself, don't yer? [*But* LEM *makes no reply, does not seem to hear the question, walks out left after his men.* SMITHERS *looks after him with contemptuous scorn.*] Stupid as 'ogs, the lot of 'em! Blarsted niggers!

[*The curtain falls.*]